MILLENNIUM MODERN

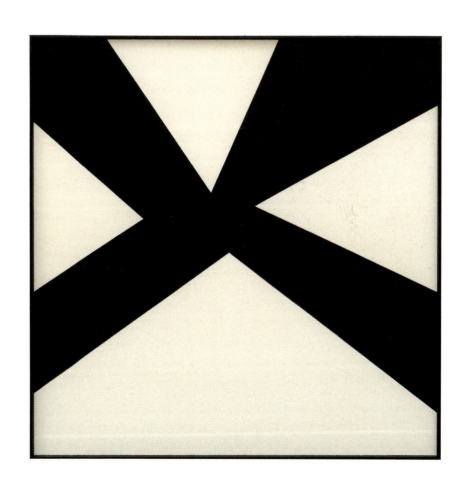

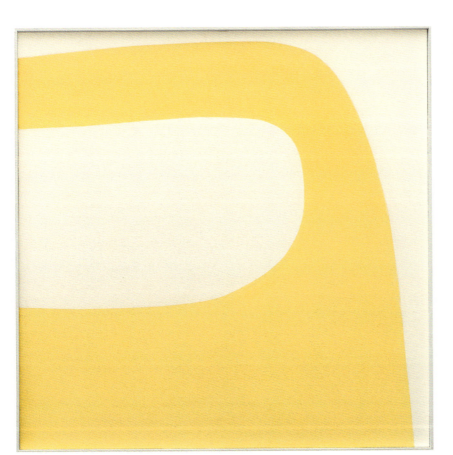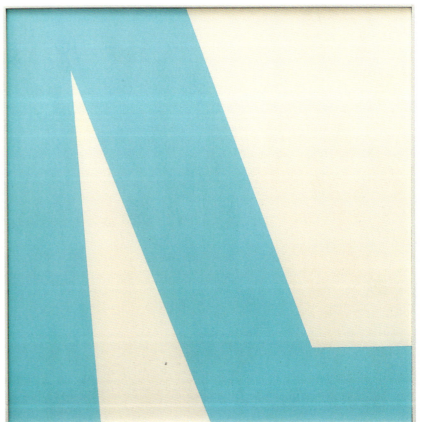

MILLENNIUM MODERN

Living in Design

Michael Boyd

Edited by Michael Webb
Foreword by Roman Alonso

with additional contributions by
Christopher Farr, Thomas S. Hines,
Brooke Hodge, Alba Kane,
Mark Lee and James Zemaitis

PREVIOUS SPREADS
Paintings by Michael Boyd, acrylic on wood, 2015.
Page 1 *Black Cross*; Page 2 *Green Curve*, *Red River*;
Page 3 *Banana Drift*, *Blue Turn*; Page 4 *Earth Orb*,
Plum G; Page 5 *Red Intersection*

THIS PAGE
Oscar Niemeyer, Strick House, 1964, *Hawk* chair for
PLANEfurniture, 2013, and *Earth Box Runner* rug
for Christopher Farr, 2008

NOTE
In all subsequent captions artworks, furniture and
rugs are by Michael Boyd, unless otherwise credited

Contents

8	**Foreword** Roman Alonso	
10	**Introduction** Michael Webb	

Collecting Design

| 15 | **A New Form of Gesamtkunstwerk**
James Zemaitis |
| 16 | **Hunting and Gathering**
Michael Boyd |

Restoring Modernist Houses

27	**Preserving and Expanding the Legacy** Brooke Hodge
28	**Spatial Design and the Music of Architecture** Michael Boyd
32	A. Quincy Jones Nordlinger House #1, 1948
46	William Wurster Helen D. Rich House, 1940
62	Craig Ellwood Steinman House, 1956
74	Richard Neutra Wirin House, 1949
82	**Treasuring Art and Living** Michael Webb
86	Oscar Niemeyer Strick House, 1964
108	Thornton Ladd House for a Writer, 1965
116	Paul Rudolph Rudolph Townhouse, 1975

Building on the Past

| 132 | **Case Study Revisited**
Michael Webb |
| 134 | Shed House, 2016 |

Rethinking the Chair

172	**Enlightened Citizen** Thomas S. Hines
173	**Our Time and All-Time** Mark Lee
175	**Minimalism with Soul** Michael Webb
181	**Sitting in Silence** Michael Boyd

Standing on Abstraction

| 233 | **Looking Forward**
Christopher Farr |

Collaborating with Commune

| 254 | **Ever Present**
Correspondance with Alba Kane |

Enhancing Museums

274	Sitting on the Edge
280	Birth of the Cool
286	Tisch Museum
292	Wende Museum
296	**The Wende Museum + Michael Boyd** Justin Jampol
302	**Nomadic Constructions: Saving Jean Prouvé** Michael Boyd

Landscaping Outdoor Rooms

| 315 | **Nature's Edges**
Michael Boyd |

Transcending Trend

| 344 | **Millenium Modern: Living in Design**
Michael Boyd |
| 351 | **Acknowledgments** |

Foreword

Roman Alonso
co-founder and principal,
Commune Design

Collector. Expert. Historian. Champion. Hero. Patron. Designer. All descriptions that apply to Michael Boyd in the worlds of art and design.

Collecting came first. He was a successful musician, with not only a fine-tuned ear, but a keen eye for the modern, the mind of an artist and an extraordinary and willing partner, his wife Gaby. Armed with these gifts (weapons really!) he dived into the world of design… following his heart and educating his eye, voraciously. The Boyds collected design not just to have it, but to learn from it. Eventually learning from having wasn't enough. There was a need for making. The next step was creating.

The furniture, the houses, the rugs, the objects, the art are the result of a lifetime of searching, gathering, and preserving beauty. Everything he designs is informed by his very close relationship to the 'real' thing. For years he's lived with the best in 20th-century design, and he doesn't put it in a glass case. He sits in it and plays in it and loves in it and this is what makes his work unique. It's not merely inspired by his extraordinary collection, the work is a meaningful expression of his daily life, his passions. Whether in a modernist, baroque, or colonial setting; whether in a residence, hotel or restaurant, his pieces always add intelligence and cool. They are beautifully made, and they are classic and original… like Michael.

Arrowhead lounge chairs, *Plank* armchair, *Arrowhead* conversation bench, installed at Farmshop Marin for Commune Design.

Introduction

Michael Webb

An autodidact with strong opinions, Michael Boyd has immersed himself in the history and creativity of modernism. His faith in the fundamentals is unflinching, as is his certainty in a revisionist age. "Modernism is a philosophical approach based on rationality and reality," he declares. "It grew out of the visual chaos of the 19th century in a quest for honesty, simplicity, and truth in materials." He shares the idealistic vision of the pioneers and has stayed true to their principles in his own work even as modernism has evolved from a narrow torrent into a broad stream with many tributaries.

For him, design is a second career following a highly successful stint as a composer for movies, television shows and commercials. Over the past forty years he has become ever more ambitious and accomplished as a collector, restorer, artist, designer, and landscaper. All of these activities are interrelated as part of a holistic vision, and each has informed the others. Some have been solitary endeavors; many have been collaborations with skilled artisans, architects, clients and peers. In *Candide*, that timeless satirical novel, Voltaire urged us to cultivate our gardens, and Michael has heeded that advice, figuratively and literally.

In the twenty years I've known him, I've tracked his achievements and obsessions, writing about houses he has restored and furniture he has designed. I am in awe of his skill in spotting buried treasure: the one significant piece, scarred and begrimed, that emerges from a pile of junk. He has the eye and the experience that every connoisseur needs to distinguish between a rare original and a convincing copy. And he has put these finds to good use in furnishing rooms and serving everyday needs. The rooms he and his wife, Gabrielle, create for themselves and a few lucky clients are intensely livable. The objects may be museum-quality but there are no taboos on touching and sitting. A curator might cringe, but the furniture has held up well: it was, after all, designed for use, not show.

I share Michael's commitment to rigor and purity, and his deep aversion to surface decoration and the self-indulgent excesses of post-modernism. But my tastes are more eclectic and we enjoy arguing about the contemporary scene. Often, I catch a whiff of the revolutionary fervor that inspired the polemics of Le Corbusier and the Bauhaus instructors. For him, modernism ended around 1965; I insist that it never went away. There is good and bad work in every decade and many different ways in which to interpret the founding principles of modernism. But I can understand why modernist architecture was sometimes perceived as arrogant and insensitive, and how it became debased. The legacy of urban renewal and homogenous skylines is appalling. However arguable Michael's beliefs, the beauty and distinction of his work counts for much more. By limiting the scope of his interests he has intensified his focus on those seven decades of creativity and the astonishing variety of expression they contain.

His familiarity with the classics shapes the striking variations he has played on basic themes in PLANEfurniture: finely crafted chairs and tables for home and contract use. His love of hard-edged abstraction feeds into bold canvases that have now morphed into rugs. A passion for sculptural forms guides his choice of plantings as well as landscape compositions that respect nature and complement modernist buildings.

I spoke earlier of certainty. It's refreshing to encounter a skilled practitioner who harbors no doubts and has earned the right to distinguish between the exceptional and the commonplace. At a time when expertise is disparaged and every truth is questioned by know-nothings, it's important to have a few people stand up for excellence. Design is too often treated as style—an ephemeral commodity like couture. Journals and online influencers channel a craving for novelty, from advertisers and a fickle public. Michael has the old-fashioned conviction that the best designs are timeless. They never strove to be fashionable, so they will never go out of fashion. Demand for such icons may fluctuate but they will always be there.

X stools and *Plank* chairs at PLANEfurniture studio, Santa Monica

Black White Red, oil on canvas, 2001

Collecting Design

A New Form of Gesamtkunstwerk

James Zemaitis

Michael Boyd is, without question, one of the most important figures in the 20th-century design market since its inception in the early 1990s. Focusing mostly on what the art historian Nicholas Pevsner called "The Pioneers of Modernism," Michael's collection of European and American design was originally influenced by the legendary dealers Ulrich Fiedler and Barry Friedman, who first began presenting designers such as Breuer, Rietveld and Mollino in 1980s gallery exhibitions in New York and Europe. Michael added a West Coast "Eames Era" aesthetic, epitomized by such hipster collecting categories as Mackintosh amplifiers and Architectural Pottery to the highbrow European modernist traditions exhibited by Barry and Ulrich. In partnership with his wife Gabrielle, Michael acquired a series of important modern residential homes by well-known architects, and created a new form of *Gesamtkunstwerk* by restoring these residences and then filling them with his collections and stunning libraries.

At its peak, Michael's collection seemed almost endless. He had hundreds of tubular steel Thonet chairs stored in warehouses, herds of Eames pony skin LCWs, a studio's worth of vintage guitars and a seemingly limitless supply of anthropological artifacts which epitomized the decorating tradition of European artists from Brancusi to Finn Juhl. He never had just one first edition monograph on Bart van der Leck. He somehow had six copies, which led to a concept, a series of single-owner auctions which marketed his connoisseurship to a global audience of collectors and museum curators.

A typical Boyd auction would have six-figure masterworks by Mollino, Chareau, and Gray, a section of art objects which could only be assembled by one man with a terrific eye and thousands of hours spent picking at dealers in Palm Springs and Venice Beach, Paris and New York, and hundreds of books, periodicals and exhibition posters which rivaled the holdings of the finest antiquarian dealers in the world.

Our gallery R & Company probably has a half dozen important chairs in our inventory at any time with the Boyd provenance. And Michael, also a furniture designer himself, is represented as creator as we have several of his chairs in our permanent collection. There is no one else out there like Michael Boyd.

Hunting and Gathering

Michael Boyd

I have always been a collector. It's a personality type. A collector is naturally inclined towards researching and sorting, but above all, narrative building. A collector is part gatherer, part orchestrator. I was a composer for film and television for twenty-five years and collected modernist design from an early age as a hobby. Somewhere along the way, my vocation and hobby switched. With this reversal, I now restore modernist architecture, and design what I hope are sympathetic interiors, rugs, and gardens professionally, while continuing to write and play music as a hobby. The artifacts I've collected inspire my designs and help to furnish the interiors.

For me, hunting and gathering has always been more about inspiration than treasure. Every picker has a credo. Every picker has a chance. The hunt itself can be thrill enough with no objects gained. The late Julius Shulman, an architectural photographer who defined the image of liveable modern architecture in southern California, carried a Richard Neutra boomerang chair in his car when he went to shoot that architect's projects. As vintage modern furniture hunters in the '80s and '90s, we all said to ourselves "I've never found one of those, yet there are so many in the pictures." Turns out there were only a couple of other examples besides the one Shulman was toting around.

We all pored over the images in books to maybe find the rare cantilevered Dan Johnson chair we thought we had turned up. "There it is on the patio of that Case Study House!"—a triumphant moment. Other moments are not so grand. I easily tire of a piece that lacks authenticity or fails to sustain interest over time. The ideas and concepts that hover above the object have more lasting value and require less storage space. Something taking up space needs to earn it.

It is instructive to trace the evolution of progressive design from its roots in the European reform movements of the late 19th century. The craft-driven German Werkbund and its sibling in Vienna—associations of like-minded artists—laid a foundation for the Bauhaus and parallel initiatives, from Paris to Moscow. In the two decades after the Second World War the torch passed to the US, but extraordinary work emerged from Italy, France, Denmark and Finland. Those are now accepted major sources, but one can also stumble onto stellar far-flung pieces from Japan, Brazil and Norway. It is the research before and after the hunt, the restoration and use, that reward the diligent chair-chaser. Finding the right spot in an interior (or garden for that matter) for the new find can present another challenge. But the best progressive design is always in demand.

Art can be anything. Design must function; that's the principal difference between the two endeavors (if one needs to make the distinction). That is not to say that a rare Raymond Loewy vacuum cleaner needs

Clockwise from left: Marcel Breuer for Thonet, *B55* chair, 1932; *Wassily* chair (first version), c.1925; *B8* stool, 1930

OPPOSITE
(Clockwise) Pierre Chareau, side table, c.1927; Gerrit Rietveld, high back armchair, 1924/1955; Gerrit Rietveld and Piet Elling, Elling buffet, 1919/1960

THIS PAGE
(Clockwise) George Nelson and Associates, *Marshmallow* sofa, 1956; Gerrit Rietveld, *Militar* chair, 1923; Gerrit Rietveld, *Moolenbeek* chair, 1942

20

The ideas and concepts that hover above the object have more lasting value and require less storage space. Something taking up space needs to earn it.

to work. Maybe the form is worthy of a museum, maybe not; it is up to curators, writers, historians, collectors, architects and designers to decide.

The need for collecting or hoarding vintage modern has subsided now that a few enlightened firms produce and distribute elegant designs at affordable prices. But the hunt goes on. There are new trends to buck, not follow; there are timeless truths that peer from behind insensitive coats of paint or alleged "improvements" on flea-market vendor's blankets. Salvage is a way of life. Looking and imagining—and reimagining—is never ending. Used or new, garbage to some, treasure to you—the gathering and organizing, repairing and revisiting, is like planting trees—it makes the world a better place.

Whether your find is an architectural masterwork by a big-name designer, or an anonymous design object of some visual value but no known origin, it's all part of the quest, the coordinated escape from the mundane.

The hills of California are no longer a good source for gold. Better these days to head out to flea markets, thrift stores, big and small auctions, and second-hand shops. Try not to be distracted by shiny objects and reflections; keep an eye out for humble yet interesting pieces that may have wandered out of 901 Washington Boulevard in Venice, where the Eameses had their office, or the subtle glint of a Bob Stocksdale or James Prestini hand-turned wooden bowl. Pursuing the hush of abandoned beauty can become a lifetime's pursuit.

OPPOSITE
Josef Hoffmann, side table for Wiener Werkstatte, c.1905; Arne Jacobson, *Seagull* armchair for Fritz Hansen, 1958

NEXT SPREAD
Jean Prouvé, Banquette, c.1950, Bridge Director's chair, c.1950, *Standard* chair, 1950

Otto Wagner, stool for Postal Savings Bank for Thonet, c.1904; Josef Hoffmann, stool for Wiener Werkstatte, c.1905

22

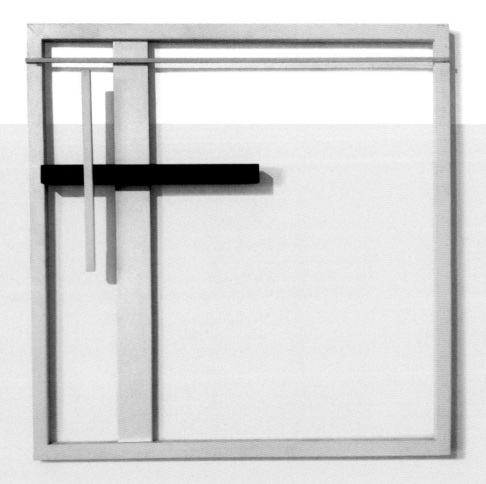

Untitled Construction, oil on wood, 1991

Restoring Modernist Houses

Preserving and Expanding the Legacy

Brooke Hodge

I first met Michael in 2003 when he and his wife Gabrielle welcomed me to their Oscar Niemeyer-designed home in Santa Monica. Not only was I awestruck by the beauty of the house and their design collection, I was bowled over by Michael's vast library of architecture and design books. These collections inspired him to become a talented designer in his own right. More recently, Michael's passion for design has extended to preserving and expanding the legacy of important mid-century architects including Craig Ellwood and A. Quincy Jones. I visited Michael and Gaby at Jones's 1948 Nordlinger House #1 last year and was so grateful that their impeccable restoration of the house would preserve it for decades to come. With *Millennium Modern: Living in Design*, Michael's talent and passion will no doubt influence a new generation of architects and designers.

A. Quincy Jones, Nordlinger House #1, 1948, Bel Air, California

Spatial Design and the Music of Architecture

Michael Boyd

The work I do has never really changed, even though my job description has; it is all about *spatial design*. There's a strong affinity between the organization of musical space and architectural space. They both have movement within grids and the ability to go outside of them. I have designed both kinds of space and have found myself thinking in related terms: vertical (harmony in music, wall in architecture), and horizontal (rhythm in music, and floor or roof, in architecture). The clearest illustration of this shared, descriptive language is that the most-used words in my professional vocabulary are, in both music and architecture: *scale, interval, ratio, relationship, composition, structure, space, theme, passage, dimension, harmony, dynamics*, and so on…

In the Bay Area, when I was working as a professional composer, I restored several mid-century vernacular houses. Reworking post-and-beam 1950s houses was good for practice in the field, but with all of the resources and time required, I wished for something more meaningful. I always dreamed of working on a historically important modernist building: to make it breathe again—and then to live in it. I was chasing not only the resurrection of a modern house's former glory, I wanted to live in design.

My quest eventually brought me, along with my wife Gabrielle and two understanding sons, Sam and Henry, to the Paul Rudolph townhouse on Beekman Place in New York City. There was something exhilarating about this multi-level interior. But what started out appearing as a powerful, if slightly theatrical, piece of architecture, began to feel like an endless fugue of experimentation. As time passed the triplex reminded me of musical exercises and scales—not finished, cogent work. Nothing was fixed: as a laboratory it was intriguing, but as a living environment for a family it was less successful. Someone calculated that the Rudolph apartment alone had twenty-seven different levels in addition to the stairs, and I began to think that this was about twenty too many! This first-hand experience of living in architectural design that was more complicated than necessary had a profound impact, and made me daydream of Case Study Houses, their stark beauty glistening in gorgeous settings.

Ultimately I came to see that my deepest conviction was directed towards simplicity, not complexity and profusion for its own sake. The most sublime musical passages have fewer notes and the composer makes each one count. The adagio, slower musical movements, allow beauty to linger. I value direct and pure design in music and architecture over cleverness or flash. Just because you *can* do something does not mean you *should*; technical facility for its own sake is perhaps the most misguided endeavor. I reflected upon having an uncomfortable domestic stint at the Rudolph house and why that was, and how that experience initiated my obsession to seek out restraint

A. Quincy Jones, Nordlinger House #1

and calm. More than anything else, I could see firsthand the benefits of a clear path to function and the abbreviation of form(s). My family had conducted the experiment; we lived in this dazzling design. In the end, the Rudolph maze was vertigo-inspiring and obfuscated more than it clarified. Paola Antonelli, who spent a lot of time in the building with us, referred to it as a "beautiful nightmare".

As we made our way west again to follow the sun-seeking dream—a vision of humble flat-roof homes in the desert-by-the-sea (e.g. A. Quincy Jones' Crestwood Hills neighborhood)—we found we could relax again. I settled into work, restoring the Strick House by Oscar Niemeyer and working on several Neutra, Ellwood, Lautner and Schindler houses in Los Angeles. I realized I was thinking about music once again; I returned to my favorite themes in music and buildings: openness, airiness, neutrality—the reduction of expression. I gravitate towards the sonorous, away from cacophony or discord. Adagio is always my preferred tempo; I want to take my time inventorying the slow movement, traveling calmly through a cloud of restrained chords and melody. It has become a one-note samba: in all design, try to *use fewer notes and make them count* as displayed in the atmospheric trumpet solos of Miles Davis. The serene lyrical passages of Debussy's *La Mer*, the stability and regular rhythm of Ravel's *Bolero,* or the divine micro-music of eccentric French composer Erik Satie, resonated more deeply for me than the dense and challenging harmony and rhythm of, say, Schoenberg or Stravinsky. In today's parlance, Frank Zappa is intriguing as a philosopher and cult figure but I cannot exactly bring myself to listen to the actual songs. Mark Twain observed that Richard Wagner's music was "not as bad as it sounds." Difficult works of art are one thing if it is a piece of music passing through time, or a painting or chair that can be put into storage, but quite another issue when the work has the permanence, weight, and scale of architecture.

My family was so contented in the Niemeyer house, with its inspiring combination of modernity and modesty that we decided to stay. At that point it made sense to begin restoring buildings and their interior and exterior environments for other people, so I could continue the work without disrupting family life. I take pride in debunking myths about modernism for my clients. There is a widely held belief that living in design (amidst modernism) means that you are stuck in a sterile box. Although both Le Corbusier and Neutra referred to their houses as machines, they never prescribed that occupants should live like machines. The homes were intended to be frames for living. In *Making LA Modern: Craig Ellwood, Myth, Man, Designer,* a book I edited a few years ago, I consciously emphasized the warmth of Craig Ellwood projects rather than their utopian philosophy or hard edges.

I value direct and pure design in music and architecture over cleverness or flash.

Peter Zumthor uses the word *atmosphere* in architecture to convey gravitas and boundless sweep, much like Jon Hassell's celestial muted-trumpet melodic motif or phrase suggests the eternal. My serenity stems from creating a sheltered interior inside of a strict piece of modernist architecture. The trick is to achieve a balance between discipline and rigor on the one hand, and humanity and intimacy on the other. At the Strick House we installed palm-wood floors to infuse a stronger sense of the exotic spirit of Niemeyer and Brazil. We referenced the lush tropical gardens of Roberto Burle Marx, Niemeyer's frequent collaborator, for the restoration of the landscape, reaching for the ethereal.

In restoring modernist houses I do whatever is necessary but with as little intervention as I can manage; a John Cage approach to building reconstruction. Absence and omission are my go-to tools. I try to make the architecture, interior, and landscape, literally sing, and live again, by establishing (or re-establishing) a dialog between all these disciplines. I always try to leave the least detectable trace of my presence, to be invisible ideally—but I can never pull it off completely.

As with the restoration of a painting or the composing of a wall of ambient music, the desired goal is total transparency. The best impression I could possibly leave behind would be if—after laborious and time-consuming work on a piece of architecture—it appeared as though I was never there. It is of course understandable that architects want to put their own design program forward, but I prefer to operate as close to *zero* as possible—a desirable condition Mies called "almost nothing".

Sometimes documentation is missing, and I am forced to make educated guesses. In those situations, I strive for what Schindler referred to as an "interesting plainness". I found that I was able to absorb and digest an architect's style, and then reconstitute it, just as I had done in the music industry. In the world of commercial music composition, one of my areas of specialty was capturing the essence of historical recordings—complete with patina and authentic, stylistic nuances—and extending the language into new work.

Now, in reclaiming architecture, I do the same: I process style and extrapolate the visual vocabulary of an architect—the unique handling of mass and void and the particular sense of spatial organization. Yet there are times when I am forced to improvise, to riff. Often there is not a drawing for a certain aspect or area of the project, or the plans bear no relation to what was actually built. Rudolph, for example, would submit permits to planning boards, and once they were approved, go on to execute something totally different. He was bored. I was scrambling. I do need to fill in details on these types of occasions and I try to channel the creator the best that I can. I tune-in to stylistic consistency in design as I do in music. But sometimes my task is to

A. Quincy Jones, Nordlinger House #1

accommodate new or future needs. Again I ask myself "what would the architect see or say?"

Charles Eames said, "don't try to be original, build on something that really works". This is more than a folksy quip—it is a way out, a clue to solving almost all problems of design, especially if you give up on the idea that new is always an improvement. My argument is for deep quality over invention for its own sake. I try to follow the logic of modernist systems already elegantly laid out. Innovation and progress are not my main pursuits in my involvement with architecture or music —universality and truth are, or at the very least, a sense of inevitability and correctness. The music in architecture is there if we listen for it, telling us to dial down our crosstalk and let these eternal truths direct decision making. For me, music is most divine when it is open; architecture and design are most inspiring when they are simple. In the final analysis, you need to *feel* it, like tempo. It's a groove to get into, a mood that gives more space than it occupies. My aim is to revive these architectural works invisibly so they can survive to be appreciated by future generations. I want their lessons to be available to all, their total design to be as beautiful moving forward as it was when it was newly born.

A. Quincy Jones
Nordlinger House #1

1948, Bel Air, CA
Restoration completed 2020

This was Jones's first residential commission for a client. The influence of Frank Lloyd Wright is evident in the angularity of the plan, the horizontal sweep and the flared redwood cladding. Extensively glazed living spaces sit atop a recessed street-level garage and a projecting bedroom wing is elevated on a steep slope. When restoration work began, the pool had been buried in the rear yard and the structure had been neglected for decades. Working with original drawings from the UCLA Archive, Boyd restored the original configuration, editing out layered additions in the breakfast area and adding back the built-in L-sofa. He refreshed the exposed brick hearth, cabinetry and stepped ceilings, along with an open staircase and period fittings. The exterior redwood had deteriorated too far to be left in its raw state, so this was sanded and painted the soft gray that Jones used on some of his later houses. The gardens by Garrett Eckbo were also restored and rejuvenated, with new plantings and a pool added to the grounds.

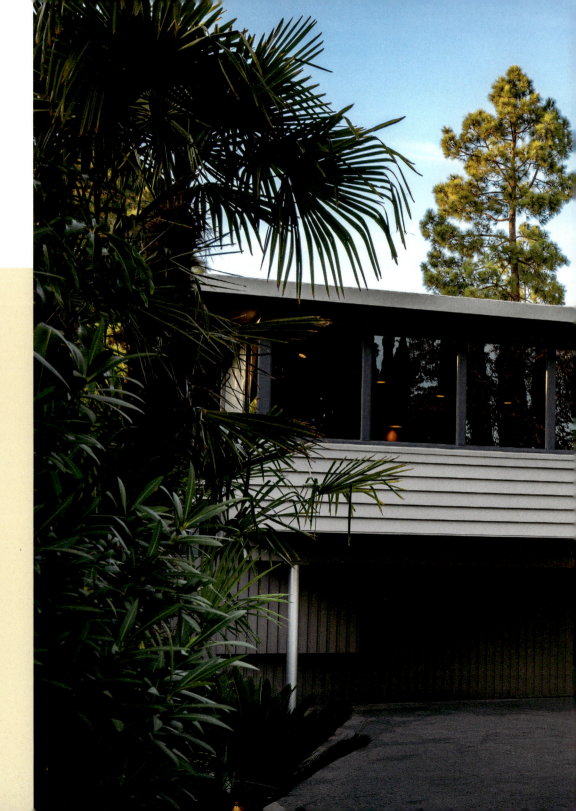

Frank Lloyd Wright cube stool, c.1950;
Charles & Ray Eames, *LAR* chairs, 1950

Ray Eames, *Time-Life* stools, 1960; *Tortoise* table for PLANEfurniture, 2016

Charles & Ray Eames, *DSX* side chairs, 1950; Carlo Mollino, table for Café del Sole, Cervinia, 1953

Charles & Ray Eames, custom *LTR* stools, c.1950

Grasshopper bar stools for PLANEfurniture, 2019

Charles & Ray Eames, *Cat's Cradle* chairs, 1950

NEXT SPREAD
Arrowhead lounge chairs, *Brasilia* table, *Little Mountain* chairs, all for PLANEfurniture

William Wurster
Helen D. Rich House

1940, San Francisco, CA
Restoration completed 2018

Located on Telegraph Hill in San Francisco, this house has the character of a modernist European villa, with its stuccoed concrete walls and tight spiral staircases. Its purity had been compromised by later owners and the principal task was to return the house to its original condition, while incorporating some necessary updates. The task was complicated by the insensitive intervention of an architect in the Wurster office in 1980. Black bull-nose marble counters gave the kitchen and bathrooms a funereal air, and the bleached Philippine mahogany that Wurster had specified for the counters was used all over the bedrooms and window frames. Guided by drawings and plans from the Wurster archives at UC Berkeley, Boyd repurposed the mahogany to replace the marble counters, and recreated the soft, light-filled interiors that Wurster intended. The original layout was restored to open up a sweeping view from the Bay Bridge to the Golden Gate Bridge. An interior garden by Thomas Church, restored by Boyd, creates a modern urban indoor/outdoor experience—to the extent that the San Francisco climate allows.

VKG copper chairs and table, c.1948; Jean Prouvé, *Standard* chairs, c.1950

LEFT
Donald Judd, galvanized arm chair (one of two extant); Charlotte Periand, stools, c.1950; Jean Prouvé, *Visiteur* chair, 1952

NEXT SPREAD
Jean Prouvé, *Standard* chairs, *EM* table, stool, all 1950; Alexander Noll, wood objects, 1950s; Francois Stahly, bronze sculpture, 1950s

PAGE 54
Master bedroom: John Mclaughlin, painting *Untitled*, 1957; Le Corbusier, *Totem* lithograph, 1963; Jean Prouvé, African table, c.1950

PAGE 55
Donald Judd, *Swiss Box*,1987; Jean Prouvé, sideboard, c.1950

PAGES 56-7
Master bathroom

PAGE 58
Serge Mouille light, c.1950; Jean Prouvé, free form table, c.1950; Karpen of California, Horn chair, 1950

PAGE 59
Jean Prouvé, *Toute bois* chairs, c.1950, *Antony* desk, and stool, c. 1950; Hans Bellman, sofa, 1950s

THIS SPREAD
Jean Prouvé, benches and table from Electricité de France, Marcoule, c.1954

Craig Ellwood
Steinman House

1956, Malibu, CA
Restoration completed 2010

In the mid-1950s, even a schoolteacher could afford an acre of land overlooking the Pacific and commission a frugal, wood-framed, glass-walled residence from a firm that was winning acclaim for its steel-framed Case Study Houses. The Steinman house had survived intact beneath a shroud of untamed foliage, and Boyd launched a three-year campaign to realize its potential for new owners. Within the house, carpeting laid over the concrete slab was replaced by cork, and all the surfaces were cleaned and refreshed. The challenge was to select furnishings of the right scale, period, and refinement, without turning the interior into a time capsule. Ellwood design principal Jerry Lomax had added a detached carport in 1960 and remodeled the former garage as a children's room. To balance the composition, Boyd designed a pool cabana of similar size on the opposite side. The cabana, pool and palm trees create an outdoor living area that extends the house into the landscape.

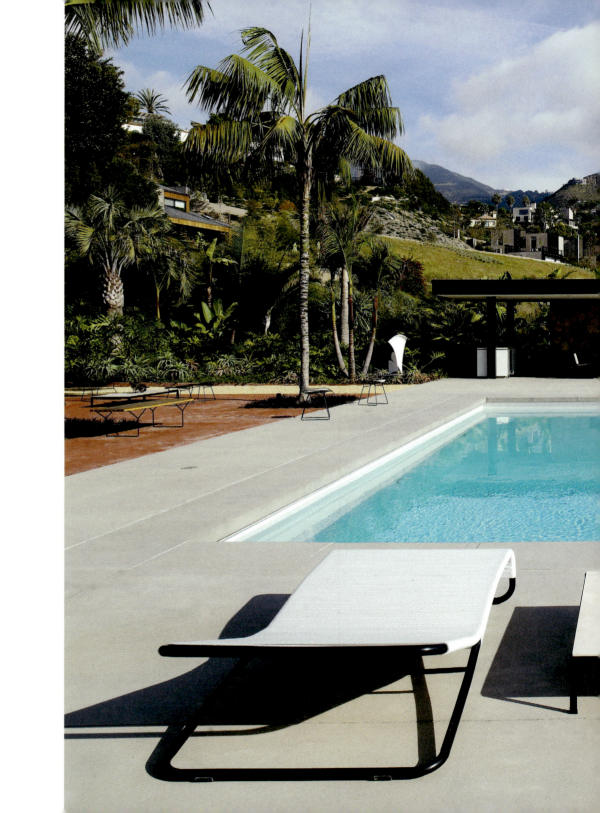

Pool and cabana: Van Keppel-Green furniture

Charles & Ray Eames, *LCM* chairs, 1946; Paolo Piva, coffee table for B & B Italia, 1970s; Katavolos, Little & Kelly, sofa model *8/FC* and stools for Laverne International, 1953

E1 rug for Christopher Farr, 2010

Florence Knoll, sofa, 1954; Gilbert Watrous, lamp for Heifetz, 1951; Poul Kjaerholm, *PK61* table for Fritz Hansen, 1955; Karl Blossfeldt photographs

73

Richard Neutra
Wirin House

1949, Los Feliz, CA
Restoration completed 2010

The restoring of the Richard Neutra Wirin House, from 1949, was performed with Mark Haddawy, another expert in the field of modernist architecture restoration. Located in the Los Feliz hills, across the street from Frank Lloyd Wright's Ennis-Brown House, the Wirin House is sited on a sharply sloped lot. Neutra's solution of having the building hug the site as it descends results in an elegant dualism. From the approach above, the architecture is strongly horizontal, with a view of downtown Los Angeles visible from above the roof line. From the pool and gardens below, the architecture is boldly vertical and melts seamlessly into the cascading grounds. A disagreement between Neutra and the original owners over the removal of a tree resulted in the landscape design never being executed. The 1940s Neutra documented plans have now been fully realized, including the free-form walkway at the entrance from the street to the front door. The split level residence affords views from all elevations, of the gardens, neighboring trees and surrounding structures. Clear Douglas fir was used to replace deteriorated case work and an updated version of the linoleum was used to refresh the floor surfaces. The outer form of the building belies the intricate geometries within; the stairwell to the lower quarters and the details at the exterior deck railing are expressive, far from rectilinear. Boyd and Haddawy created Neutra-inspired furniture and rugs to articulate the space. Vintage Eames and Neutra furniture was also installed, giving the home an air of authentic modern comfort. The cabin-like feel of the Wirin House is a departure from Neutra's purist International Style architecture, like the Von Sternberg or Kaufman houses; the design is informed by the rugged and mountainous site.

N1 rug for Christopher Farr, 2009

N2 rug for Christopher Farr, 2009; Arteluce, three-arm lamp, c.1960

Michael Boyd *N1* rug for Christopher Farr, 2009; Richard Neutra, armchair, 1930s/c.1990

Michael Boyd and Mark Haddawy, custom hassocks, custom table, 2009

Treasuring Art and Living

Michael Webb

Architect-designed modernist houses stand out from the crowd of tract housing and, like bespoke suits, they are usually tailored to the needs and tastes of a demanding client. When the owners move out or move on, such a house often becomes an orphan. It may be sold at a premium because of its pedigree, but this in no way protects it from insensitive alteration or even demolition. Only a fool would buy a valuable painting and then cut a strip off the canvas to make it a better fit for the bedroom wall, have it overpainted to match the sofa, or wantonly destroy it. Anyone doing so would be denounced as a philistine and shunned by artists and dealers. But classic houses constantly succumb to such ignorance and greed.

That's because art has a sacred aura, while even the best architecture is considered expendable. There may be a public outcry when a landmark—like New York's Penn Station or Frank Lloyd Wright's Larkin Building in Buffalo—is demolished, but houses are private property and are thus off the radar. Protests went unheeded when developers leveled the Joseph von Sternberg house of Richard Neutra and the Dodge House of Irving Gill, both undisputed masterworks. The buyer's only concern was to profit from the development of the site; the existing house was a mere encumbrance.

Neutra's Kaufmann and Miller houses became decrepit and might easily have been lost, even though Palm Springs is one of the few American cities that cherishes modernism. His Maslon House in neighboring Rancho Mirage was demolished overnight by a purchaser who wanted to spite the previous owners. The Strick House was put up for sale with no mention of Oscar Niemeyer and was rescued from demolition at the last moment.

More insidious is the fate of modestly scaled houses that are wrenched out of shape or radically rebuilt by owners who are fixated on size, for themselves or for resale. The Case Study House that Eero Saarinen and Charles Eames designed for John Entenza was submerged within a crass addition. Craig Ellwood's CSH #17 was later obscured by a faux classical façade grafted onto the original glass and steel, and his CSH #18 was similarly disfigured. Thornton Ladd's House for a Writer in Santa Barbara, which Boyd restored in 2002, is now unrecognizable. One could extend the list indefinitely.

It is this loss and abuse of an artistic legacy that inspires Boyd to conserve whatever he can and to replace what has been lost, much like a surgeon operating on a sick patient. Like humans, houses fall victim to the ravages of time and a lack of care. Structures fail, materials wear out, and luster fades. The Kaufmann house shriveled under the assault of the desert sun and had to be stripped to its bones and reconstructed from new wood, aluminum and field stone which were carefully matched to the original. Ellwood's Hunt House,

> "What really constitutes an architectural atmosphere? This singular density and mood, this feeling of presence, well-being, harmony, beauty... under whose spell I experience what I otherwise would not experience in precisely this way."
> —Peter Zumthor

Strick House, Gerrit Rietveld, *Moolenbeek* arm chair, 1942; Frank Lloyd Wright, occasional table, c.1950

perched above the Pacific in Malibu, appeared shabby but essentially sound when it was re-photographed a few years ago. Soon after, expert restorers discovered that parts of it were on the verge of collapse.

Boyd arrived one morning to begin work on a Neutra House near UCLA and found that the owner had, in the short time since their last meeting, re-plastered and painted the house in a mac 'n' cheese orange inspired by a recent trip to Tuscany. The plaster was smooth-troweled and sloped at the base, like the vernacular rustic buildings he had seen. Fortunately, Boyd had a copy of the original Neutra specifications and was able to persuade his client that the house should be restored to its original white, sand-finished stucco with crisp edges and clean corners. There was an outpouring of gratitude from local aficionados of modern architecture.

Doctors take an oath to do no harm, and anyone restoring a significant building should do the same. Like a living creature, it has matured over the years and its character has been enriched by age. Patina—in a house or on a credenza—is the equivalent of silver hair. Shiny surfaces and the latest appliances are the hallmarks of a contemporary kitchen, but they look out of place in a vintage modernist house. I've clung to the kitchen that the Eameses used eighty years ago in my Neutra apartment, with its original tiles, cabinetry and O'Keefe and Merritt stove, and have declined offers to botox it. Houses can be over-restored, and a recent transformation of Neutra's Kun House felt unreal in its glossy perfection. I'm reminded of a comment by the artist Chuck Arnoldi, who said "I like faces that wrinkle when they smile, not Stepford wives."

One of the key choices to be made in restoration is between purism—seeking total authenticity regardless of cost—and the pragmatism of accepting scuffed surfaces, vintage fittings, and intelligent substitutions. It is between this purist and pragmatist approach that Boyd turns to atmosphere and patina, and he sets himself to the task of pulling out the unique DNA and aura of each space. As Peter Zumthor speaks of atmosphere: "What really constitutes an architectural atmosphere? This singular density and mood, this feeling of presence, well-being, harmony, beauty ... under whose spell I experience what I otherwise would not experience in precisely this way."

Perfection is often unaffordable and unachievable. A preservation society in Massachusetts discovered this when they acquired the house that Walter Gropius built for his family in 1938. They could hire skilled carpenters to restore a Colonial house using time-honored tools and techniques, but Gropius wanted his house to be a showcase of the latest materials and some of these were no longer in production. The new custodians had to substitute for the next best thing where they could no longer save the old.

The Getty Modern Architecture Initiative was faced with the same challenge in its conservation of the Eames House and Studio. They had to find a new version of the synthetic floor tiles that were cracked beyond recovery and decide how to protect the furnishings from sunlight beaming in through expansive single glazing, while continuing to allow visitors to peer inside.

These are a few of the issues that confront Boyd whenever he embarks on a restoration project. Like the original architect, he's working for a client or his own family, so there's a dialogue that determines the program and the budget. In southern California, where most of these houses are located, one has to contend with unstable ground, especially in the hills, and tough seismic regulations. Foundations and the physical structure have to be secured and that is often the major expense.

Building codes in California have become so exigent that many older buildings would not be approved today. Some of Schindler's low-budget houses are perched on steep hillsides and are slowly subsiding under their own weight. Frank Lloyd Wright's textile block houses are as porous as sponges and require constant attention to keep them stable and weatherproof.

To secure a tax concession under the Mills Act, the restoration has to conform to exacting rules. Once a house has received a historic listing the exterior cannot be changed, and any interventions must be reversible and conform to the Department of the Interior's stringent standards.

Boyd has honed his skills over twenty-five years and learned from his experience as a resident of six radically different houses and apartments, developing his own distinctive approach to the work of architects he reveres. Each project has its own possibilities and constraints, but the guiding principles are the same: a mix of purism and pragmatism, inspiration and compromise. These houses are living environments as well as works of art, and both deserve equal consideration. "There's a mix of responsibility and freedom," he observes. "Custodians of important buildings must be cautious and diligent, but they should also remember the architect's intention to promote health, happiness, and ease of living."

"Restoration involves peeling back insensitive layers of additions and re-workings, getting into the mindset of the original designer, and extrapolating with care, thought and delicacy", he continues. "There are plenty of standard procedures on our job sites. Hardware is stored and numbered. Original doors, case goods, windows and vintage fixtures are saved, catalogued and restored non-invasively whenever possible. Hairline cracks in stone and concrete are always accepted unless the structure is deemed unsound."

Once the fabric and finishes of the house have been refurbished, there comes the question of installing the latest technologies—which may soon be superseded. Air conditioning conduits have to be inserted intravenously into thin walls. Few were concerned with energy conservation through the 1960s; now it has become a pressing issue and it may be necessary to add an invisible layer of insulation and substitute a higher grade of glass.

Anyone living in a vintage house has to accept small bathrooms and kitchens, but these can be subtly enhanced to make them more appealing, and a spare room can be transformed into a walk-in closet. The goal is to provide modern conveniences while retaining the integrity of the original. It's essential to make a house work efficiently and to satisfy contemporary expectations if it's to survive intact and be cherished by future generations.

When the restoration is complete, Boyd sometimes has to step away and focus on the next job if he is not doing the interior. The new owners may have ideas of their own and pursue a very different aesthetic. Boyd has resigned himself to this. He is fond of citing Le Corbusier's experience in Chandigarh, the new capital that the architect designed for the Punjab province of

India. Asked if he was dismayed by the fact that the exterior decks, so carefully calibrated and planned by his office were now, some years later, filled with bicycles and personal clutter, he responded with a shrug: "Life is always right."

OPPOSITE
Helen D. Rich House

THIS PAGE
Strick House: Charlotte Perriand *Maison du Mexique* shelving unit, 1952; André Bloc, *Bellevue* chair, 1951; Josef Hoffmann, metal basket for Wiener Werkstätte, c.1905

Oscar Niemeyer
Strick House

1964, Santa Monica, CA
Restoration completed 2006

The Strick House is a T-plan International Style house that is radically different from the curvilinear designs for which the architect is best known. The Boyds bought it in 2003 on the eve of its destruction from a developer who wanted to replace it with a faux Tuscan mega-mansion. It took nearly three years to restore the fabric of the house and surround it with tropical landscaping inspired by the gardens of Roberto Burle Marx, a close associate of Niemeyer. Vertical aluminum louvres, admired by Niemeyer himself, were added to the street façade for shade and privacy, and exterior red bricks were painted white for a more international feel. The garage and upstairs apartments were remodeled to serve as a double-height library and showcase for the owners' collection. Within, linoleum and wall-to-wall carpet was replaced by palm-wood flooring, but every effort was made to conserve the original kitchen and bathrooms. The interiors were furnished with an eclectic mix of classic modern furniture, African tribal art, and Boyd's abstract canvases. Niemeyer, upon seeing the photographs of the results of the Strick House restoration, said "it's nice to finally meet this house. I like the way you have restored it to its 1960s elegance."

87

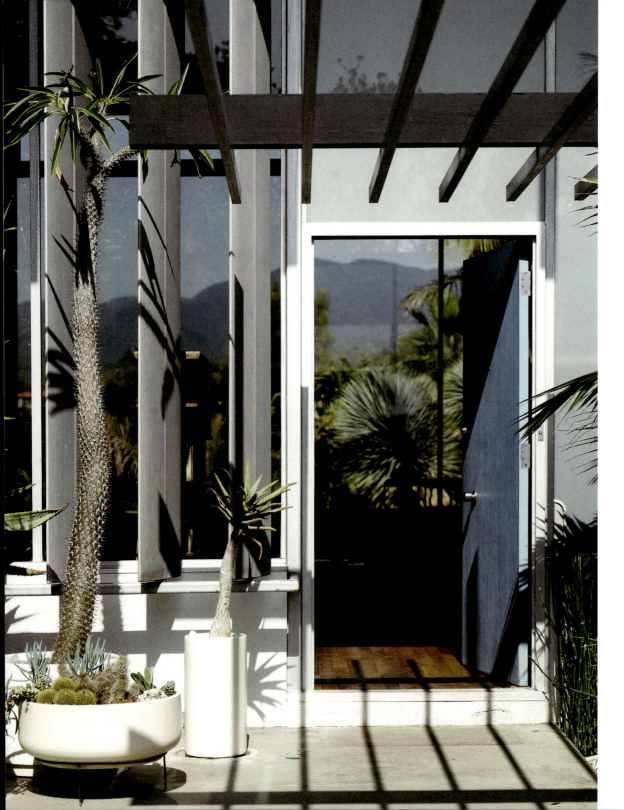

Oscar Niemeyer, lounge chairs and ottomans for the Paris Communist Party headquarters, c.1970; Serge Mouille, ceiling light fixture, c.1950; Burgoyne Diller, painting, *First Theme*, 1959-60; Man Ray sculpture, 1950s; George Nelson, *Marshmallow* sofa, 1956; Frederick Kiesler, free-form tables; Donald Judd, *Swiss Box*, 1987; Marcel Breuer, bentwood nesting tables for Isokon, 1936; George Nelson, rosewood *Thin Edge* cabinet, 1952

PAGE 95
Pierre Chapo, free-form table, c.1950; Robert Mallet-Stevens, armchairs, c.1928

THIS PAGE
Eero Saarinen, *Tulip* stools, 1956; George Nelson, *Ball* clock for Howard Miller, 1947

OPPOSITE
Jean Prouvé, *Visiteur* chair, 1952; Le Corbusier, *LC 14* stool, 1952; John McLaughlin, *Untitled*, 1957

Jean Prouvé, free-form table, c.1950; Jean Burkhalter, armchair, c.1930

OPPOSITE
Carlo Mollino, carved wood side chair, 1953; Josef Hoffmann, side table for Wiener Werkstätte, c.1905; Otto Wagner, stool from Postal Savings Bank, Vienna, c.1904

OPPOSITE
Master bedroom, George Nelson, *Coconut* chairs, 1956; Isamu Noguchi, *Fin* stool, c.1946, *Rocking Stool and Table*, 1948

Van Keppel-Green Chairs, c.1950; Architectural Pottery, c.1950

Thornton Ladd
House for a Writer

1965, Santa Barbara, CA
Restoration completed 2002

Located near the Mission in a Spanish-themed city, this steel and glass pavilion by Thornton Ladd and his partner John Field Kelsey uses the language of the Case Study Houses. Impressed by the residence Ladd built for his mother in Pasadena, Boyd researched the architect's other work and discovered that he was living in retirement in Ojai. Excitedly, he sought advice but was rebuffed. "I have no interest in the revival of the past," wrote Ladd. "It reminds me of difficult clients and a useless chase of relevance. I am now entirely absorbed in Eastern thought and religion." Undeterred, Boyd restored the house to its original condition for the use of his own family. The moss green terrazzo floors were heavily damaged by an overlay of carpet; every nail hole was painstakingly filled. A gigantic chandelier and gaudy Buddha sculpture were auctioned off and the proceeds paid for the removal of these inappropriate additions. Boyd's family enjoyed their retreat and the proximity of the ocean, before moving on to the Strick House.

OPPOSITE
Clockwise from top: Arne Jacobsen, *Egg* and *Swan* chairs, both 1958, and 3300 series sofa, 1956; Charles & Ray Eames, *Surfboard* table, 1951; Frank Gehry, *Wiggle* stool, 1972; Sori Yanagi, *Butterfly* stool, 1954; Hans Wegner, *Ox* chair and ottoman, 1960; Eero Saarinen, *Tulip* side table, 1957

PAGE 112
Charles & Ray Eames, custom dining table, 1956, and side chairs, 1950

PAGE 113
Isamu Noguchi, *IN-50* table, 1947; Gilbert Watrous, lamp for Heifetz, 1951, George Nelson, rosewood *Thin Edge* cabinet, 1952

Paul Rudolph
Rudolph Townhouse

1975, New York City, NY
Restoration completed 2001

The multi-level penthouse that Rudolph added to a Beaux-Arts apartment block offers a sweeping view of the East River and was cantilevered out over Beekman Place to the dismay of his neighbor, Mrs. John. D. Rockefeller. A three-dimensional labyrinth of interlocking volumes that recalled Rudolph's Art + Architecture Building at Yale, it became a laboratory that he tinkered with right up to his death in 1997. When Boyd began to restore it, he consulted architects from the Rudolph office that had worked on the project originally. But they wanted to do things their own way, and Boyd decided to trust his own judgement. "We navigated carefully through the levels of urban archeology and came up with a legible, livable solution," he recalls. "Since all the mirrored mylar had to be removed from the steel beams for restoration, we decided at that point to play down the Studio 54 version of the building's history while amplifying the elegance of the white marble and steel incarnation, alluding to Rudolph's original vision and his legacy of purist modernism in Florida."

THIS PAGE
Mies van der Rohe, *MR20* armchair for Thonet, 1927

OPPOSITE BOTTOM
Master bedroom: Bart van der Leck desk, c.1925;
Gerrit Rietveld, *Militar* chair, 1923; Marcel Breuer,
aluminum armchair, 1932-33

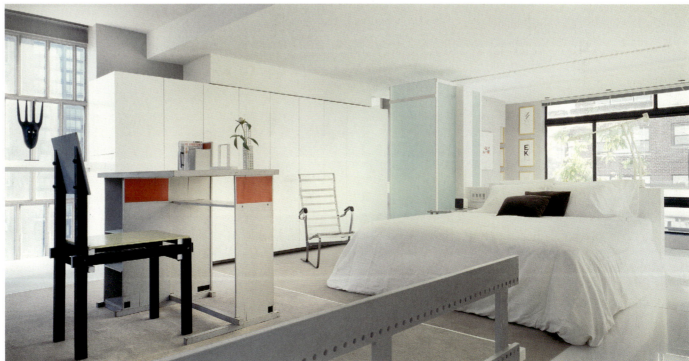

Library chairs by Gio Ponti for Montecatini Building, Milan, 1936; Jean Prouvé, *Banquette No. 356*, 1954

OPPOSITE
Library annex: Gerrit Rietveld, high back arm chair, c.1924/1950; Serge Mouille standing lamp, 1952

PAGE 126
Clockwise from left: Gerrit Rietveld, *Red/Blue Chair*, 1918/1965; R.M. Schindler, side chair from the Lechner House, 1946; Jean Prouvé, *Antony* dhair, 1954; Frank Gehry, *Wiggle* stool, 1972; Marcel Breuer, slatted arm chair, 1924; Alvar Aalto, armchair *No. 31*, c.1934; Josef Hoffmann, *Sitzmaschine*, 1905; Willy Guhl, fibrated-concrete rocking chair, 1954; painting by Myron Stout; Roger Tallon, *Bata* stool, c.1977

PAGE 127
Gerrit Rietveld and Piet Elling, *Elling Buffet*, 1919/1960; Gerrit Rietveld *Berlin Chair*, 1923

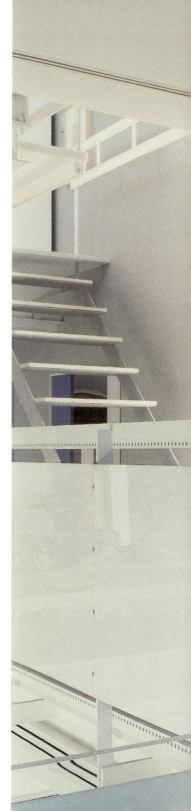

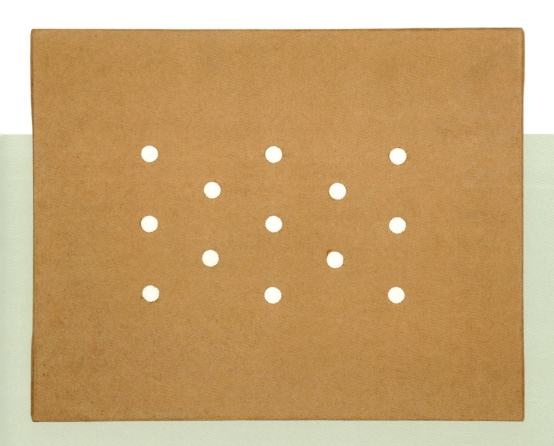

Dots, 1998, assemblage, cardboard, painted plywood

Building on the Past

Case Study Revisited

Michael Webb

Shed House is the first ground-up residence Boyd has designed, working with Laurel Broughton. They had collaborated on the pool and cabana at the 1956 Ellwood Steinman House, when Broughton made the construction drawings of Boyd's concepts.

The 6000-square-foot house in the Malibu hills is deceptively simple. A long bar of rooms clad in gray-stained boards intersects a white stucco block to form a T. Both wings have monopitch roofs, which tilt up to reveal treetops and mountains, and down to frame the ocean a quarter mile away. They give the house its name and impart a sense of motion. It's a fusion of architecture and nature, rooted in the luxuriant landscaping, and contrasting sharply with the showy mansions that jut from neighboring hilltops.

For the client and his wife, it was a huge leap from their historic house in Old Town, Alexandria, Virginia, although they had often summered beside the Pacific. Inspired by an article on a Craig Ellwood house that Boyd had restored, they decided they would enjoy a change of style and scenery, so they wrote to ask if he could find them another modern classic in Malibu. It proved a fruitless quest, and they grew tired of waiting. As Boyd recalls, "one evening over dinner, the client said, 'why don't you design it yourself?' and, after a moment of pause, I said 'that's a great idea.'"

Boyd found a run-down 1950s bungalow on a gently sloping acre of land and fixed it up as a temporary retreat for the clients while he and Broughton developed their ideas for the house that would replace it. "Before we tore it down, we saw how well it was sited, and we located the new indoor-outdoor fireplace at exactly the same point to preserve a memory of the old," says Boyd. He raised the pad about 18 inches to give the new house a better view of the ocean, and decided on a T-plan, similar to that of the Strick House.

Boyd describes his concept: "I wanted to capture the soul of the Case Study Program and its many variations, from the rigor of Craig Ellwood's California Classicism to the casual quality of William Wurster's soft modernism… I tried to push the ideas in those houses even further, stripping down and adding warmth. I was also thinking of the conceptual clarity of the iPhone. My brother is a professor of electrical engineering at Stanford and we share in our work, if nothing else, a love of elegant solutions."

The client gave Boyd a free hand but stipulated that the roofs should slope. "I grew up in a small Michigan town, living in a flat-roofed house and I soon discovered that they are prone to leak—even in a dry climate," the client observes. Boyd accepted the challenge, and the complementary angles of the roofs on each wing create a lively dialog.

The entry is recessed to reveal the free-standing fireplace, which serves as a marker, and is clad in shimmering Heath tiles. It draws you into the living room

"I wanted to capture the soul of the Case Study program and its many variations, from the rigor of Craig Ellwood to the casual quality of William Wurster."

Michael Boyd (in collaboration with Laurel Broughton), Shed House, 2016, Malibu

and out through glass sliders to the pool terrace on the south side. The master suite looks over the pool to the ocean, and guest bedrooms occupy the north and west ends. Throughout, there's a sense of openness; of spaces flowing through the house as freely as the ocean breezes.

Anticipating a delay in securing permits, Boyd installed new plantings at the outset. In his own house and commissions across the city, he has honed his skills in creating green architecture, using trees and shrubs as organic sculptures, strategically placed to complement windows and walls. Mists from the ocean nurture palms and bamboo, birds of paradise and other subtropical shrubs, which blur the boundaries of the site. Brightly colored steel sculptures emerge from dense plantings in the kitchen garden like tigers in a Douanier Rousseau painting.

Varied textures and tones enrich the simple forms. The gray cladding boards are sandblasted and wire-brushed, and the sand finish of the white stucco catches the light. Floorboards of stained French oak scattered with rugs complement the narrower oak boards of the ceilings, which are parchment-glazed in the main block and silver-gray in the flanking wing. The walls at either end of the living room are painted aluminum, and the study niche at the mid-point is clad in grass cloth.

Designing the interiors spurred Boyd to create his own furniture. He transformed salvaged sliding doors of old-growth Douglas fir from the bungalow into the first *Plank* chairs, and that was the seed of PLANEfurniture, a range that now comprises a hundred variations on 25 basic designs. In Shed House, PLANEfurniture alternates with a few vintage American and European finds, as well as the clients' growing collection of contemporary art. The spareness of the furnishings makes every detail stand out clearly. For Boyd, this is a manifesto. "In the deluge of choices that confront us today, editing is a viable option for creation," he explains. "Building on the innovations of the past can bring us renewal for the future."

Shed House

2016, Malibu, CA

Entry: *Crab* table for PLANEfurniture, 2013, aluminum free-form tables, 2013; Danny Ho Fong, *Lotus* chairs, c.1960

OPPOSITE
Charles & Ray Eames Sofa, Compact, 1954; *Paddle* arm chair, 2013; George Nakashima, splay-leg table, 1948

THIS PAGE
Paddle armchair for PLANEfurniture, 2013; George Nakashima, splay-leg table for Knoll, 1948; Charles & Ray Eames, *LTR* tables, 1950

PAGE 149
Arrowhead corded lounge chair, 2012, and *Plank* chairs, 2012, for PLANEfurniture and custom *Plank* dining table, 2014

152

Harry Bertoia, *Bird* chair and ottoman, 1952

OPPOSITE
Sting Ray stool for PLANEfurniture, 2013; Andy Warhol, *Space Fruit: Oranges* screen print, 1978

Tall Block stools for PLANEfurniture, 2015

Florence Knoll hanging cabinet, 1958; *Plank* armchair and *Bird* bowl for PLANEfurniture, 2011

Master bedroom: *Arrowhead* bench for PLANEfurniture, 2012; Arne Jacobsen, *Visor* lamps for Louis Poulsen, 1958

Mountain chaise, 2013, *Flip Lounge* chairs, 2012, side chairs, 2012, all for PLANEfurniture

Raw, 1994, assemblage, painted steel,
Douglas fir plywood

Rethinking the Chair

Enlightened Citizen

Thomas S. Hines

Many good designers seem to know from the beginning that design is their mission in life, and they pursue it with a monastic concentration. Later, after becoming professional designers, they may continue this focused existence, but their success also gives them the time and courage to branch out and explore the world—even the world of other designers whom they might have previously seen as competitors. They get interested in the history of design and of the other arts and they become engaged and enlightened citizens of the world. Michael Boyd has reversed this progression. After a good liberal education at the University of California, Berkeley, where his parents taught, his success as a commercial music composer allowed him to focus on his intense connoisseurship of the arts, particularly of buildings, books and furniture. Now he himself has become a designer of all of those, especially furniture. His striking new work contains memories of, affinities with, and homages to such masters as Rietveld, Breuer, and Schindler, but the design voice is his own. Bravo to life's reversals!

Our Time and All-Time

Mark Lee

Philip Guston once commented that when you begin working on a painting, there are a lot of people in the studio with you—your teachers, your friends, family, painters from history, critics. One by one they leave, and eventually, if you are lucky, you leave too. Michael Boyd's PLANEfurniture series is born of a creative process not unlike the one described by Guston. After decades of collecting, studying, and being immersed in the scholarship of modern furniture Michael Boyd is creating furniture of his own. When looking at the pieces made of rudimentary planes, one could sense and deduce their historical lineage while remaining wholly original; an originality that evolved through erudition. If one has to imagine the process of how their forms came into being in Michael Boyd's studio, one could tell that Rietveld was there, Schindler was there, Judd was there; but one by one, they all left the studio. And all that is left are the beautiful pieces that are of our time and of all time.

ROD series side chair for PLANEfurniture, 2012

Minimalism with Soul

Michael Webb

PLANEfurniture is a timeless product for troubled times. The optimism, invention, and frugality that carried America through the Great Depression, the Second World War and its aftermath, are embodied in these fresh interpretations of basic principles. They strip away the superfluous to support and serve their users, elegantly and economically.

Inspired by the pioneers of modern design, these pieces have good proportions and a simple beauty. Each is composed of a few elements, cut from a sheet of wood and assembled to achieve an interplay of shapes and angles.

Charles Eames was once asked if the idea for his molded plywood chairs had come to him in a flash. "Yes—a thirty-year flash," he responded. Everything he had ever done—tinkering with a camera as a boy, struggling as an architect in the Depression, teaching at Cranbrook, conceiving a new kind of chair, and shaping plywood for military uses—made possible the rapid realization of an enduring design that did more with less. Boyd would never compare himself to one of the great originals, but the designs for PLANEfurniture that he sketched and refined in months were nurtured over many years.

The quest for elusive treasures and his skill in deploying them intensified Boyd's passion for truth and beauty in design and inspired him to make modest contributions of his own. PLANEfurniture is the expression of an aesthetic philosophy and the insights he has gained as a connoisseur.

Just as white contains the full spectrum of colors, so is simplicity the distillation of complexity. That is why the Eames plywood chairs still look fresh, nearly seventy years after they were first conceived, along with the best designs of Mies, Breuer, Prouvé, Jacobsen, Aalto and Saarinen. All these form-givers were architects, who designed furniture for their own buildings, treating both as an equal challenge.

Mies believed it was harder to design a great chair than a great building, and it's easy to see why. It must provide comfortable support for the human body, which comes in a variety of shapes and sizes, without sagging or toppling; it should be durable, portable, and offer good value. To join the pantheon, it needs to have a strong personality and a timeless grace. Each of these architect-designers achieved those goals, not once but repeatedly, and it would be absurd to tamper with their classics.

Other architects, artists and craftsmen treated furniture, and especially the chair, as a laboratory in which to test ideological principles. Often, they created a one-off and moved on to another task, leaving the object as an undeveloped prototype or as a singular work of art. Some of these historic artifacts have been reproduced and marketed, often losing the characteristics that made them unique. The planar chair of Gerrit

Arrowhead perforated side chair for PLANEfurniture, 1991, Corian

"When an object is reduced to its essentials, proportions come alive and simplicity takes on its own resonance and character."
—John Pawson, *Minimum*

Rietveld, in natural or painted wood, began life as a hand-crafted experiment in form. Reissues of the *Red/Blue Chair* with their slick finishes and primary colors preserve the idea but betray the spirit of the original. R.M. Schindler has been more fortunate. His roughly assembled plywood furniture and built-ins are cherished by a few collectors and still enrich some of his houses, but their raw quality has deterred others from reproducing them. At the opposite extreme, Donald Judd designed a few wooden chairs, tables and stools as useful sculptures and they are still fabricated to the same exacting standards as his art works.

In contrast to the formal perfection of the first group, the experiments (even the impeccably finished Judd pieces) provide an opportunity to take good ideas further and play variations on basic themes. It is here, and in the humble work of anonymous designers, that Boyd has found his inspiration. An earlier generation of innovators was more concerned with the process than the product; for them, furniture served as a three-dimensional sketch pad, and the forms led on to something else. For Boyd, the goal is not to invent for its own sake, but to tailor and edit. As Mark Lee observes, there are echoes of favorite designers in PLANEfurniture, but the four groups each has its own identity. They go back to basics and combine simple shapes in new ways.

The *Plank* series is the most uncompromising. Four flat planes are invisibly joined to create a chair that is as elemental as a child's drawing. Each plane is set at an angle to its neighbor to form a bold X in profile and the illusion of a ledge jutting from a tilted plank at the front. It is simultaneously a geometric sculpture that stands apart, and a surprisingly comfortable place to sit. (You are reminded that a kimono is assembled from a few rectangles of fabric that adjust to the contours of the user.) Stools and side tables complement the chairs. Every piece is made to order in a wide variety of woods and painted finishes. Backs can be perforated and tailored cushions added.

None has as powerful an impact as the basic side chair made from old-growth Douglas fir. The boldness of the grain recalls the patterned marbles that Adolf Loos, a sworn enemy of applied ornament, used to enrich his luxurious interiors. Like rosewood, old-growth fir is now a protected species, but it can be scavenged from the closet doors of vintage modern houses, and Boyd is constantly searching for salvaged sheets. Traces of the paint that concealed it remain as reminders of its secret life as the wood reveals its natural pattern and tactility for the first time.

The *Wedge* series has a softer, more traditional character and may see wider distribution as a result. Slatted lounge chairs, ottomans and benches are christened *Arrowhead* for the profile of their members, and mahogany versions have a strong affinity to the classic Adirondack patio furniture. The differences are equally significant. *Arrowhead* pieces are like a well-tailored jacket of rough tweed: rugged yet refined, familiar in outline but elegantly detailed and much more compact than traditional models. A lounge chair has a corded back and seat, and the holes for the cords are staggered to create a subtle pattern around the edges. A side chair appears at first glance to be a sensuous version of the *Plank* chair, until you notice the details: a back that is rounded to conform to the width of the seat, and then flares out below like a well-cut shirtwaister. And the wedge supports differ in width from front to back, establishing a rhythm in the profile of the chair.

For the *Rod* series, Boyd was inspired by a crudely shaped chair of unknown origin that he found while foraging in Berkeley. The original may have been made in a backyard workshop by a handyman with a welding torch; the new version takes the steel rod for a promenade, defining a graceful frame to support the seat and back. The contrast of black rod and white cords, rounded corners and interlocking planes, gives this piece a surreal quality that marks it off from its peers. It comes as a side chair, an ottoman and a lounge chair that can be flipped to vary the angle of the seat.

The *Block* series could be seen as Boyd's homage to De Stijl in its asymmetrical geometry and its juxtaposition of planes and square rods defining surfaces

JF Chen exhibition: *Michael Boyd, CONTINUUM*, 2016

and volumes. Half closed, half open, *Block* tables come in varying heights, but employ the same wood elements for each. Unlike the chairs, where the components and the outline are pared to a minimum, the *Block* series represents a layering of parts, and an elaboration of the assembly.

Soon after the launch of the planar furniture in 2012—in the *types + prototypes* exhibition at *Edward Cella Art + Architecture* in Los Angeles—Boyd felt the urge to counterpoint the biomorphic with the rectilinear. Anthropomorphic and curvilinear forms cried out for exploration. "I tried to channel Alexander Calder and Jean Arp, and began drawing mountains and bodies of water," he recalls.

Out of these sketches emerged the throne-like *Hammerhead* chair, the elegantly sculptured *Hawk* chair, and the sensuously carved *Tortoise* stool. The shapes are enhanced by the rich grain of walnut and wengé wood. A stand-out is the *Bat* chair, whose spiky, patinated bronze frame has a moody presence that evokes the sculptures of Lynn Chadwick. The two waves are distinct but complementary, providing a richly varied family of pieces to furnish public and private spaces.

Color is another variable. All the pieces can be hand-painted, using a matte Dutch marine paint in subtle or vibrant tones. That provides an alternative to the natural grain and further emphasizes the angularity of the chairs and tables. As Schindler observed, "a beautiful plainness is the most precious and difficult thing to achieve." The softest green or the brightest red share the plainness that comes from a focus on the essentials, and the absence of decoration and whimsy. That's for the users to supply. Furniture should provide props for the drama of living, not draw attention to itself.

PLANEfurniture is a reaction to the craving for novelty and the commercial pressure to switch styles as frequently as couturiers change hemlines. Every piece sings its own song and joins in the chorus. Each shares a sensibility that borders on the primitive—a word unjustly condemned as pejorative—which can connote unconscious excellence. John Pawson found that quality in the rough glaze of a Raku tea bowl and the irregular textures of handmade paper, which are products of a craft tradition.

Boyd's furniture is made by hand, but the shapes are crisp and the surfaces smooth. The differences between these and machine-made pieces are as subtle as the stitching on a bespoke suit. This is artistry that conceals itself and offers a quiet alternative to the mass market, which pretends to offer a wide choice but has an underlying uniformity. Like the pieces the Shakers crafted, Michael Boyd's PLANEfurniture is minimalism with a soul.

Douglas fir *Arrowhead* side chairs, 1991

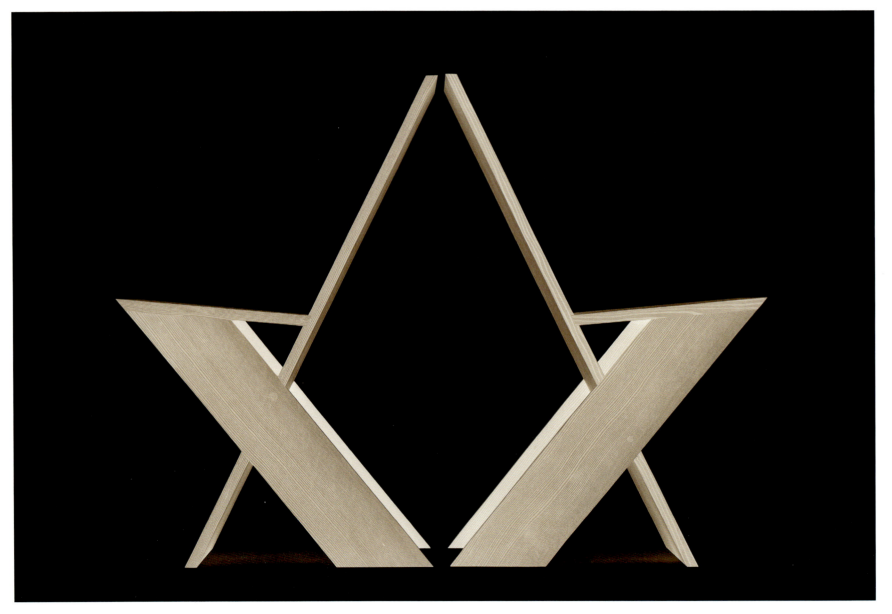

Sitting in Silence

Michael Boyd

When I first began to create interiors, and place furniture and design objects in these interiors, I sought a wider context. I wanted to zoom out as far as I could. I eventually arrived at the German concept of *Gesamtkunstwerk*—a dialogue between art, architecture, design, and landscape, building towards unity. I had been searching for this quality of universality, timelessness and totality. I had always been interested in landscape, architecture, painting, sculpture, and design, as separate issues or disciplines, but suddenly all of the forces could reinforce and inform each other, to become a total work of art.

Furniture can be a kind of micro-architecture, and buildings can feel like scaled-up cabinets or case goods. The micro-world and real world of architecture and design are identical in that the relationship of components, ratios and pitches make or break a design. It often seems that the DNA of the larger work is fully present in the smaller work and visa-versa—a phenomenon that Alison and Peter Smithson referred to as "the universe in a Mies chair."

The chair is the most omnipresent object in our domestic lives. It can be a sculpture and it can serve the human body. There are many types and prototypes, some uncomfortable but beautiful, others ergonomic and physically awkward. In any case the design of a chair has been recognized as a rite of passage for an architect or designer. There is a pantheon of great designs and many unknown or anonymous wonders. Modernism has a rich history and there are many opposing trends: the organic design of Isamu Noguchi, Jean Prouvé and Arne Jacobsen in contrast to constructivist or architectonic work by Gerrit Rietveld, Marcel Breuer and R.M. Schindler.

Although I don't believe in a hierarchy of the arts, there is a way in which furniture leads to architecture. I have had a collection of musical chairs (acquiring and letting go) because it is a lot less expensive and more logistically practical to collect chairs than buildings. The chair has been imagined and re-imagined, the territory is crowded, and surprises are few. Some are inspiring but all need to cradle or hold the body. Whether pushing boundaries or pushing buttons, the chair is a staple of design, nothing less than a point-of-view.

Rectilinear chairs telegraph order, architecture, and stasis. Anthropomorphic and biomorphic chairs suggest motion, dynamism, and wild nature. A good interior has a mix of the two. Planar plays off of biomorphic abstraction and vice-versa. Planar geometry is based in logic and sensuous form in emotion. Both are valid independently but seem empowered by the other's presence. If you remember the Julius Shulman and Ezra Stoller photographs of modernist interiors, there was almost always an abstract sculpture on top of the Florence Knoll rectilinear credenza and often

Plank chairs, 2012

a biomorphic relief on the wall of a constructivist office building or residence. It is as though one were to juxtapose canvases by Mondrian and Picasso.

Whether composing and orchestrating musical notes, plant material in a garden, or furniture placement in interiors, the designer is dealing with arrangement, balance, asymmetry or symmetry. With landscapes one has to anticipate where the canopies of plants will go in the future—at what rate, what direction of exposure, and so on. These things are not separate disciplines, but at an essential level, all the same.

One may question the need for another chair at this point and respond: as one traces their history there are some forms that seem pregnant with possibilities not yet explored. Why not continue reanimating the basic concepts of the chair? Why not consider approaches from French modernist thought filtered through California craft tradition? Why not infuse modernity with tribal art aesthetics? I always have been seduced by the soul and patina found in older things. I noticed these attributes absent in contemporary work and wanted to evoke them without faking distress or suggesting wear. I wanted pieces that felt time-honored from the start. When I got over the initial challenge of designing a chair, I tried to forget all I had learned and seen and just set myself to the task of making things.

I quickly realized that, when restoring modernist architecture and furniture, I had been working with extraordinarily talented artists and artisans who could execute my designs and ideas on a high level. I wanted to work not only in woods, bronze, plaster, and stone, but also in Corian, resin, aluminum, carbon fiber, gas injected plastics, skateboard park high-density laminates—materials of our age. Everyone I have engaged with has a wealth of experience and a dedication to their specific craft. They are the experts I go to and I always end up refining designs after our initial discussions, trying to work my way to the essence of a particular material—to understand its properties and push the limits. It is definitely a collaborative process.

My goal is that every design feel unfussy, straightforward, no tricks. It's true that a lot of effort goes into the final impression of effortlessness—just as a cinematographer goes to great pains to appear in absentia. He or she may have had to hang from a rope ladder on a helicopter, but the final result is a smooth and seamless shot for the finished film.

Usually, creators start with the wish to design for Everyman—to provide the masses with great design choices at a low cost. It rarely works out that way, unfortunately. You have to pay for fine workmanship and the best materials. Lack of distribution also can kill the noblest of concepts. The original idea for the *Plank* chair and many of the pieces from *types + prototypes* was that they be flat-shipped in a simple kit. The experts

Exhibition *types + prototypes*, Edward Cella Art + Architecture, 2012, installation view

Whether pushing boundaries or pushing buttons, the chair is a staple of design, nothing less than a point of view.

I consulted all agreed: it was not a money-saver. I shrugged, "back to the drawing board."

Some of the greatest European designers had different priorities. Josef Hoffmann created masterworks and opulent interiors for the well-to-do. Pierre Chareau, Eileen Gray, Jean-Michel Frank—in fact many of the best French Modernists—created furniture for exclusive projects. It's one of the reasons I am so engaged by the history of design. It's only after the initial hype and hyperbole die down that we actually know whether an idea has been successful or not. For me an interval of, say, thirty years is a good test of relevance.

This idea seems timely today because we live in a world of focus groups and consensus. The makers of television, advertising, and the movies do not move without first checking for a favorable response. We have to let all of the commercial, political, and socio-political jargon recede before we have any real sense of the true quality of the design of an object or the power of a work of art.

Searching for colors can be intimidating, and I can tire of it so quickly in an interior or on architecture that I spend countless hours agonizing about tones and values and their longevity. Color can be a dangerous game. So many crimes are committed in its name. The color keys that Le Corbusier developed are inspiring because there are no bad choices. Another color grail is Donald Judd's edit of the RAL chart. I have a theory that most offensive and unacceptable colors were developed after 1965—the year Le Corbusier swam out into the Mediterranean and never looked back.

Old advertisements, vintage clothing, antique electric guitars, and automobiles, are all good indexes that color can have soul and a virtually infinite shelf-life.

I have lived with the designs of Rietveld, Schindler, Wright and Judd in the constructivist idiom, and Mollino, Ponti, Arp and Jacobsen, in the anthropomorphic area. Each has its own discreet integrity. A dealer once said to me, "you will love this desk, it's Rietveld-meets-Mollino." That actually sounds like a train-wreck more than a piece of furniture I would like. I aim for immaculate design, the minimal gesture—yet always in the service of maximum concentration and impact.

As a collector, I am aware of the precedents and have a fair sense of where and when to steer clear. There are many archetypal forms in furniture that I gravitate towards: the Swiss mountain chair, the African chief's chair, the military folding chair, or the classical Greek chair. Le Corbusier did not invent the applebox stool, but he put his stamp on a refined version of it. Robsjohn-Gibbings was not the creator of the classical Greek chair, but he developed a contemporary iteration. I think my influences are self-evident to some extent. I will just say that I have always been captivated with the idea or design philosophy that hovers over an object more than the physical object itself.

Plank chair drawings, 2012

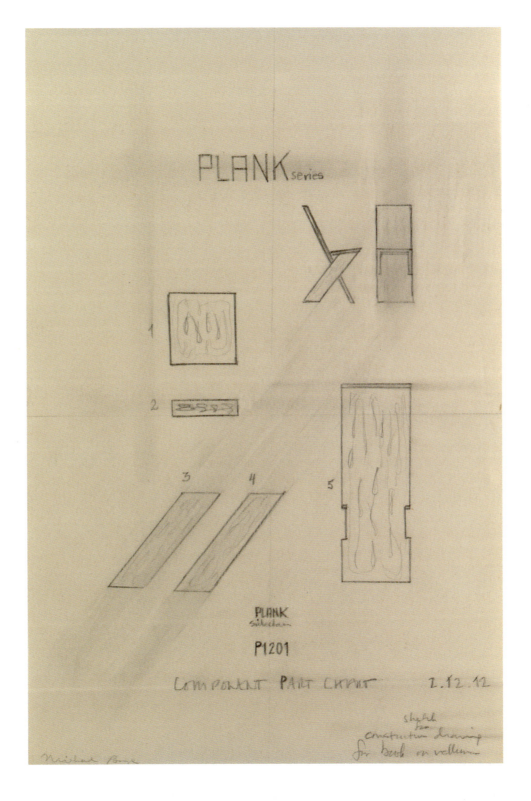

"In order to create something that functions properly—
a container, a chair, a house, it's essence has to be explored."
—Walter Gropius

Some Asian and African societies have felt no need for something like a chair and sit directly on the floor or ground. Only the ruler demanded a throne. The chair was a Western invention and always carried a loaded message. Rare materials and ornate designs were tokens of status. Today we eschew the hierarchy of decoration and deal directly with intrinsic human needs and design intent when interpreting chairs. Furniture can be used as sculptural objects of contemplation, relating to art and architecture, as well as to introduce personality or character to a room.

The Eames' *ESU* storage units and the bookshelves of Charlotte Perriand and Jean Prouvé act as buildings in miniature, and the cantilevered chairs of Mies or Breuer recall bridges and other large structural systems. One paramount achievement of the Eameses was to bring to the domestic landscape these lofty engineering concepts, in an array of seductive forms. Charles had a structuralist's orientation and was concerned with the connections where different materials met, whereas Ray began as an artist, studying under the painter Hans Hoffmann. She brought color and textural variations to the pieces, most notably to the modular group. Together they created a body of work that has endured and will never go out of style.

I try to work on design problems and constraints in a way I think is interesting and hope that others may share my interest. I always seem to be thinking about the beginnings of *design*—about what is and what is not essential. I ponder the Prouvé *Standard* chair which, along with the Eames fiberglass armchair, is one of the two forms I consider that represent the apex of modern furniture design. The elegance of the Prouvé chair is the product of sophisticated engineering made elemental. The sheet-steel frame swells out to support the body exactly and only where it needs to—and becomes attenuated where it needs to be. For decades, the *Standard* chair was denigrated as industrial or classroom furniture. Today, we see it as the climax of French style, a commodity, but it is simply an engineering exercise that has taken on new meaning because of our displacement in time, place, and context.

One cannot assign collectability to anything in advance; the limited edition is often a gallery employed, cynical market-driven device. The hardest thing for a designer to do is to remain lucid, sincere and genuine, and stay away from the clichés, touchstones and trending lighting rods. At the core of minimal design, the questions emerge: why has abbreviation held up over millennia? Why does it perennially feel new and relevant? How is it antithetical to gimmicks of all types? There is nowhere to hide rhetorically or otherwise with pure design. It feels inevitable; the heart of an idea captured convincingly, a universal solution. Sitting in silence, remaining humble in design, that's what stands up to the ultimate test. Whispering is more impactful and attractive than screaming—that fact has never changed.

Plank armchair in mahogany, 2012

Plank chair in Douglas fir, 2012

Exhibition *types + prototypes*, Edward Cella Art + Architecture, 2012, installation view

Plank chairs in Douglas fir and, opposite in painted wood, 2012

190

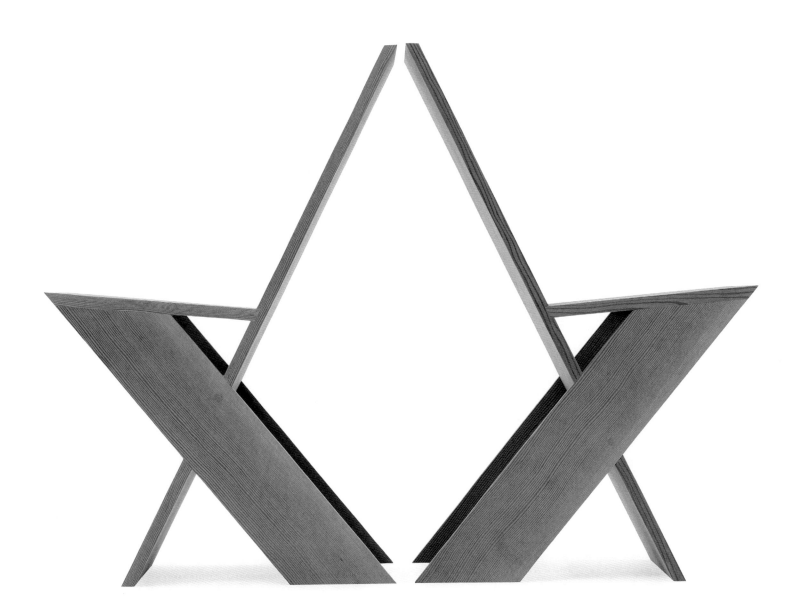

WEDGE series *Arrowhead* lounge chairs in wengé, 2012

OPPOSITE
Commune Design, Ace Hotel Downtown Los Angeles, WEDGE series *Arrowhead* chairs, 2012, custom sofa, 2014, both in ebonized oak

THIS PAGE
Plank armchair, 2012, and sofa, 2014, both in ebonized oak

3/4 *Panel* table in Douglas fir, 2010

Full *Panel* table in aluminum, 2010

ROD series, *Flip Lounge* chairs and ottomans, 2012

Johnston Marklee, Chan Luu House, Hawaii: ROD series *Flip Lounge* chairs, 2012 and *Plank* chairs, 2012

Hammerhead chair in ebony, 2013

203

OPPOSITE
Exhibition *re:Visions*, Hedge Gallery San Francisco, 2014, installation view

THIS PAGE
Hammerhead chair in ebonized oak, 2013

Stingray stools, left to right, in wengé, ebonized oak and walnut

Tortoise stool in walnut, 2013

Mountain chair, 2013, aluminum, vintage denim

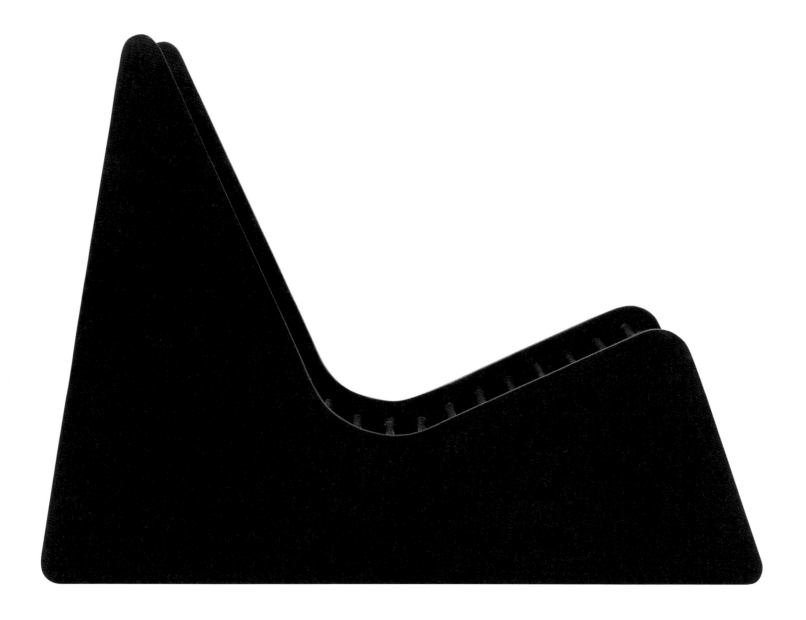

Mountain chair in ebonized oak, 2013, wood, aluminum rods

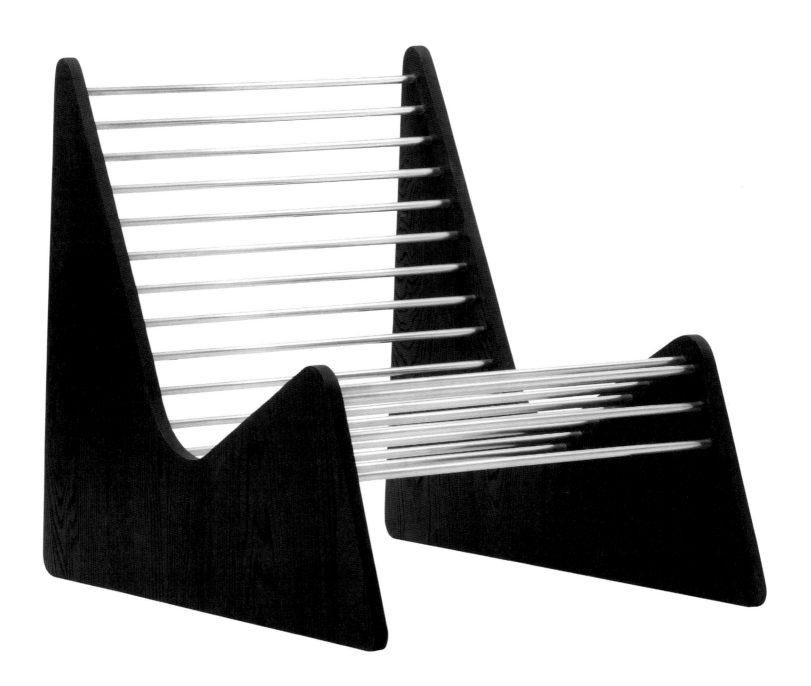

212

Paddle arm chair in ebonized oak, 2013, short paddle version

213

Paddle arm chair in ebonized oak, 2013, long paddle version

T tables in wengé veneer, 2013

215

216

Hawk stool in wengé, 2013

Hawk chair in wengé, 2013

Bat chair frame, cast bronze, 2013

Exhibition *re:Visions*, Hedge Gallery, San Francisco, *Bat* stool and chair in zebra wood, 2013. Installation view, 2014

Brasilia table in bronze and *Branch* table in wengé, 2013

Panther table in ebonized oak, 2013

Bird bowls, concrete, 2011

223

Fig bowls, 2011, bronze and Carrera marble

OPPOSITE
Bird bowl and *Fig* bowl, 2011, bronze

225

Exhibition *re:Visions*, Hedge Gallery San Francisco, 2014, installation view ROD series, *Flip Lounge* chairs, 2012

OPPOSITE
Aluminum free-form tables, 2013

NEXT SPREAD
JF Chen exhibition, *Michael Boyd, CONTINUUM*, 2016, installation view

227

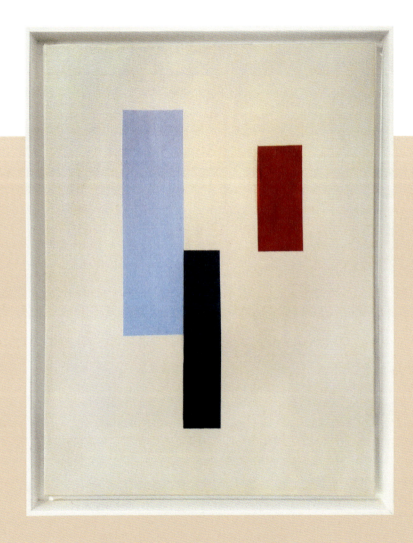

Dana Point, acrylic on canvas, 2018

Standing on Abstraction

Looking Forward

Christopher Farr

When I first met Michael and he showed me his house the only thing missing for me were rugs. That's when I first invited him to design for us as I knew he would bring to rug design his genius for form and composition. We had long discussions about Albers' color theories, the abstract paintings of Ellsworth Kelly, and the photography that informed the paintings.

Amazingly, my father's book *Design in British Industry* (Michael Farr, 1959), long out-of-print, was in his library and we talked all about the early moderns, their public struggles and private discoveries. In fact, my father's world-view of design was identical to Michael's. This modernist universe prized graceful and utilitarian solutions above all. Function first, yet beauty had its place on the next level. The beauty was defined by use and need, stripped down shape and form revealing a secret ease and refinement. Michael's own taut geometric abstract paintings felt in essence like the rug studies of Eileen Gray, and I told him so.

In 2008 I invited him to curate our 20th anniversary exhibition in London and his insights and connections made in the catalog still resonate today. He visually connected rugs with the movie sets of Jacques Tati's *Playtime*, Saul Bass' credits for Hitchcock's *North by Northwest* and also compared rugs to agricultural grain silos and city street maps.

Michael sees everything, nothing escapes his eye. In his rug designs for us, first he explored the constructivist grid, and then he exploded it. His furniture design at that time took the same turn in this path, with his initial attention to planes and Mondrianesque geometries turning to the opposing force, the languid and liquid. As Michael and I have often affirmed "no home is complete without the binary opposition of straight line and curve." Sitting in chairs together on these finished rugs we noted that you could rest on a color bar mass or melt into a void. The newest rugs hover and drift. The single-color concept is minimal but the effect of the rug in the room, in dialog with furniture and objects, has a maximum visual impact. I look forward to a continued collaboration with this unique, forward-looking designer.

Green Curve rug for Christopher Farr, 2015 in Jørn Utzon's Ahm House, 1962, London

NOTE
Michael Boyd has designed all his rugs for Christopher Farr, except where otherwise credited.

Banana Drift rug, 2015

Brasilia rug, 2015, in Oscar Niemeyer's Strick House

E1 rug, 2010, in Craig Ellwood's Steinman House

Block runner rug, 2013

OPPOSITE
N1 rug, 2009, designed for Richard Neutra's
Wirin House

Rug samples at Christopher Farr showroom, 2015, Los Angeles

Red, Black, Cream, 2007

OPPOSITE
Grey, Cream, Black, Red rug, 2007

245

246

Lozenge rug, 2007

OPPOSITE
N2 rug, designed for Richard Neutra's Wirin House

248

OPPOSITE
Dot rug, 2008

THIS PAGE
Floating Planes rug, 2013

NEXT SPREAD
Left to right: *Blue Lean* rug, *Banana Drift* rug, *Green Curve* rug, *Burgundy Mist* rug, 2015

Collaborating with Commune

Little Mountain chairs, for Commune Design, private residence in Santa Cruz, CA

Ever Present

Michael Boyd writes to Alba Kane and Commune

Hey! I feel like both you guys and I have this idea of an unfussy California-chic thing. Classic but alternative. European modernism filtered through direct approach California-craft and build tradition.

SoCal ghosts we listen to are the barefoot Schindler, sun-seeker Neutra, the radiant Eameses, as we are living in the land of Ellwood, Irving Gill, Paul Williams, and FLW… these are our heroes especially when it comes in cypress or redwood!

There is a NorCal strain too, speaking of cypress and redwood—with thinking of Luther Conover, James Prestini, and Donald Knorr… yet we also seem to always be discussing Josef Hoffmann, Otto Wagner and Vienna turn-of-the-century… focused on elegant solutions, function and glamour…

Anyway lots of influences and forefathers and mothers from the past we chat about but lots of new discovery together too in the now. Commune is ever present.

Not sure how to explain it but it is always inspiring to explore the possibilities together as a team and extended family.

The Commune details are always so interesting and beautiful and they always build on the foundation and story of the design.

With MUCH LOVE, MB

Response from Alba Kane and Commune

Hi there Michael,

I keep coming back to your idea that our Commune is *ever* present. The timing is ripe for a deep breath on this thought. The world can change in every possible way, but curiosity and imagination are ungovernable and what a relief that is. It's simple but profound, much like the ease of our communing and the products of our work.

In my attempt to define what we do together, I'm thinking about how we do it. In our studio, we always begin with the analog teachers: books, historical records, magazines. We pin pages on the walls (talk about ghosts of the past) and rely on them to take us to the spaces and places beyond our current existence. It's a process of grounding ourselves in what came before, honoring it really. Your kindred spirit does the same.

Inevitably, we are tasked with building something anew no matter how much we wish to revel in the past. We ask ourselves a deceptively simple question: how do we bring the full-grown principles of the past into the adolescent now? Michael Boyd, we think… And so it is, that we ring you up and tell you a crazy dream and ask you to design it with us.

It's you we think of when we need a chair to find itself thousands of miles away in a Kyoto hotel whispering to its occupants the stories of its California modernist

roots. It's you we turn to when we seek to explore how something designed for a suburban home in the 50s can be adapted for a bustling restaurant. It's you we look for when we need a storage room full of vintage posters. It's you we engage when we need to know the exact proportion of a Prouvé table leg. The list goes on. It's ever present.

I'll leave you with this. How lucky are we to come together in this time and place—this being the 'ever present' you mention—and to meet in the middle with our work? Ours is the kind of work gifted with both the wisdom of history and the boundlessness of discovery. I reckon this is what your mind is stumbling across as it searches to define what we do together.

These are just some thoughts on what you mean to our studio, what your artistry brings to our Commune. Your wealth of knowledge, your precision as a designer, your fearlessness as an artist, your obsessions as a curator, your love of books…they're ours too.

With immense gratitude,
Alba and Commune

Hammerhead chair in wengé in a private residence in Berkeley, California, 2016

Arrowhead side chairs in Douglas fir plywood and upholstery, originally designed for the Ace Hotel Chicago, in Roman Alonso's apartment, Los Angeles, 2018

Arrowhead lounge chairs in teak in the barbeque area at the El Centro Apartments and Bungalows, Hollywood, California, 2019

Arrowhead side chairs in Douglas fir plywood and upholstery and *Paddle* armchairs in ebonized oak and leather at the rooftop lounge of the Ace Hotel Chicago, 2017

Little Mountain lounge chairs and hand carved free form table in ebonized oak at the Ace Hotel Chicago

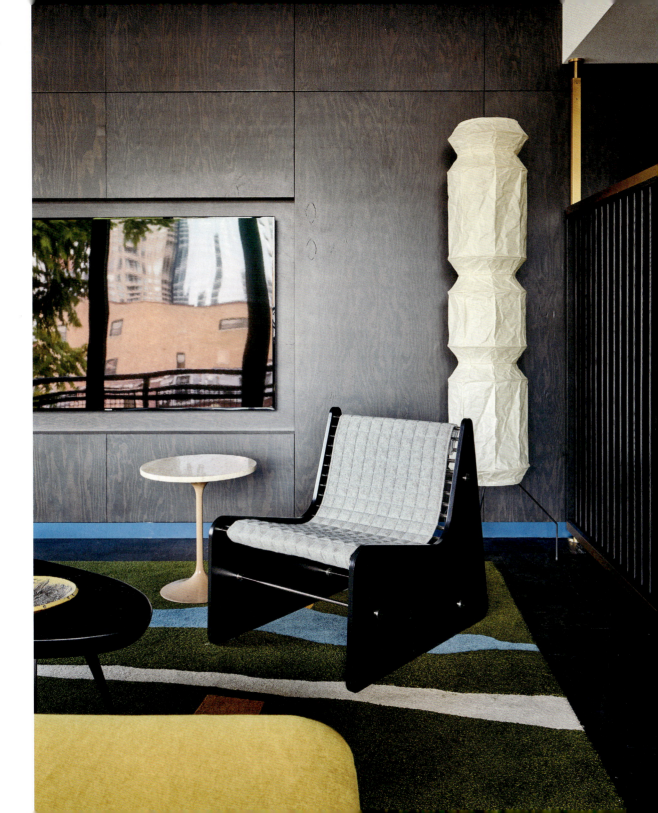

Paddle armchairs in ebonized oak and leather in the rooftop lounge of the Ace Hotel Chicago

Perforated *Plank* side chairs in the lobby of the Ace Hotel Chicago

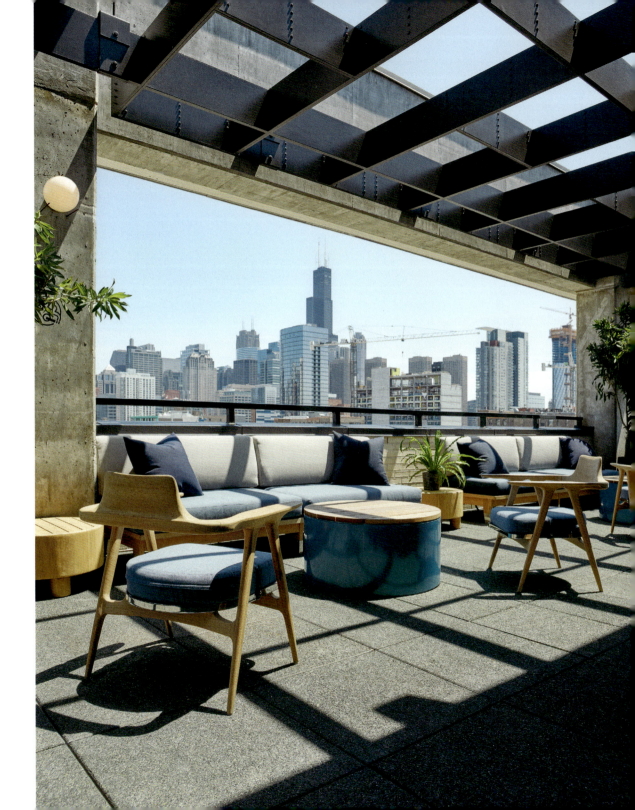

Paddle armchairs in the rooftop lounge of the Ace Hotel Chicago

Sidebar lounge chairs and *Brasilia* tables in the restaurant at Caldera House in Jackson Hole, Wyoming, 2017

Plank arm chairs, *Arrowhead* sofa and free-form ebonized coffee table in the Durham Hotel, North Carolina, 2015

Arrowhead lounge chairs and Panther tables in the lobby of the Durham Hotel, North Carolina, 2015

Perforated *Plank* side chairs at the communal table in the lobby of the American Trade Hotel in Casco Viejo, Panama City, 2013

Centered, 1995, assemblage, painted wood, aluminum, stainless steel

Enhancing Museums

Sitting on the Edge

Sitting on the Edge, the first major exhibition of the Michael and Gabrielle Boyd Collection, was organized by curator Aaron Betsky at the San Francisco Museum of Modern Art in 1998. At that time the Boyds were living in the city and had donated many pieces to the museum. For the exhibition they loaned 150 objects and pieces of furniture from their home, and the presentation was acclaimed in catalogue essays by Paola Antonelli and Philippe Garner.

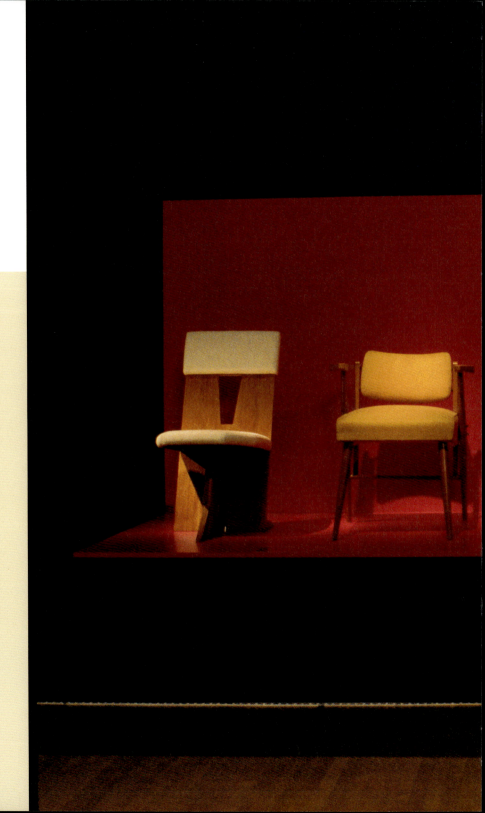

Sitting on the Edge: Modernist Design from the Collection of Michael and Gabrielle Boyd, SFMOMA, 1998: R.M. Schindler, side chair for the Lechner House, 1946; Franco Albini, pearwood arm chair, c.1955; Carlo Mollino, chair from the Casa del Sole, Ristorante Pavia, Cervinia, 1954; Max Bill three-legged chair, 1949; Jean Prouvé, *Antony* chair, 1954

PREVIOUS SPREAD
Sitting on the Edge: installation views

THIS SPREAD
Clockwise from top left: Willy Guhl, concrete chair, 1954; Edward Durell Stone, *Ozark* jute armchair, 1950; Bruce Goff, stool, c.1960; Osvaldo Borsani, *P-40* lounge chair for Tecno, 1955; Arteluce, three-arm lamp, 1952; Charlotte Perriand, *Maison de Mexique* shelving unit, 1952; Eero Saarinen, *Tulip* stool, 1956; Vladimir Kagan, custom aluminum stool, c.1960; Achille Castiglione, *Mezzadro* stool, 1957; Charles & Ray Eames, prototype dowel leg table, c.1945; Isamu Noguchi, rocking stool, 1954

Birth of the Cool

In 2008, the Orange County Museum of Art organized *Birth of the Cool*, an ambitious exhibition that traveled to other museums across the country. Named for the legendary 1950 album of jazz trumpeter Miles Davis, it chronicled the explosion of modern architecture, design and music in southern California in the 1950s. Michael curated the architecture and design portion of the exhibition drawing on his own collection and designed the installation and fixtures.

Birth of the Cool, Orange County Museum of Art, 2009, installation view

282

283

PREVIOUS SPREAD
Birth of the Cool, installation views

THIS SPREAD
Birth of the Cool: Donald Knorr, *132U* chair, 1948;
Dan Johnson, dresser, c.1950; John McLaughlin,
painting, 1950s

Tisch Museum

Architect Mark Lee, co-principal of Johnston Marklee, invited Michael to custom design some upholstered seating for the private art museum his firm built in 2016 on the Los Angeles, Paul Williams-designed estate of producer-collector Steve Tisch. In a sharp departure from the pared-down forms of PLANEfurniture, Boyd designed the sybaritic *Banana* sofa and lounge chairs—over-scaled, over-stuffed pieces that contrast with austere Donald Judd furniture at the other end of the exhibit space. The monumental *Crab* table was also designed for this private commission to complement the biomorphic abstract seating.

Johnston Marklee, *Tisch Museum*, Los Angeles: Michael Boyd, *Banana* chairs and sofa, 2014

288

290

Wende Museum

The Wende Museum explores the history of the Cold War through graphics and artifacts, from a pamphlet to chunks of the Berlin Wall. Since 2017 the museum's collections have been displayed in Culver City within a 1948 armory building. Boyd worked with Christian Kienapfel to restore and remodel the building and supervise every detail of the museum's visual package from the institution's logo to case work, from interiors to gardens, color schemes to water features. Museum director and founder Justin Jampol sets up oppositions in the collection's narrative and requested that Boyd follow suit in the revamped design package. The landscape was designed by Boyd in collaboration with the firm Segal/Shuart to be one element within the larger project that pushed aside Cold War history, and instead embraced the horticultural potential of Southern California.

The Wende Museum + Michael Boyd

Justin Jampol

No single person has had a greater impact on the success of the museum's design and spirit than Michael Boyd. He is the "building whisperer." Whereas so many architects, designers and builders fundamentally change or alter existing structures to fit their personal styles, Michael is committed to preserving the integrity of a building.

The project we first worked on together was the renovation of a former National Guard Armory in Culver City, a massive concrete building, which is now the home of the Wende Museum. From choosing the colors to designing the logo, Michael Boyd was involved in every decision along with our architect Christian Kienapfel. When others wanted to clad the exterior walls with new surfaces, Michael insisted on sandblasting the walls to expose the beautiful aggregate underneath. It was a critical decision at the right moment.

His vision for the landscaping was pure genius. Our visitors describe the garden as "magical". I had been used to a more procedural, process-oriented approach to design, but what I realized by working with Michael is that art cannot always be reduced to budgets and timelines. He found value-oriented solutions to create the visual impact of something that would otherwise cost multiple times what we could afford. It felt like a risk at the time to completely trust in Michael's vision, but it was the best decision I have ever made.

What I admire most is his advocacy for his vision. I vividly remember Michael showing up at 6am on the construction site, talking to the workers, explaining to them that their job was the most important one in the world and their attention to detail and quality would have enormous ramifications. If they did good work, they could be proud of it for the rest of their lives. He would encourage and nudge when necessary to ensure the best possible result. His passion is infectious and these otherwise surly and cynical workers were completely mesmerized. Michael won't stop until he has everyone on board.

It is my great pride and privilege to embark on a new project with Michael, in conjunction with Brian Wickersham and AUX Architecture, to transform an abandoned structure on a property adjacent to the museum, into a state-of-the-art center for the community. Once again, Michael Boyd is overseeing the design of the building, the choice of the materials, and, of course, the landscaping. And, once again, he will work his magic.

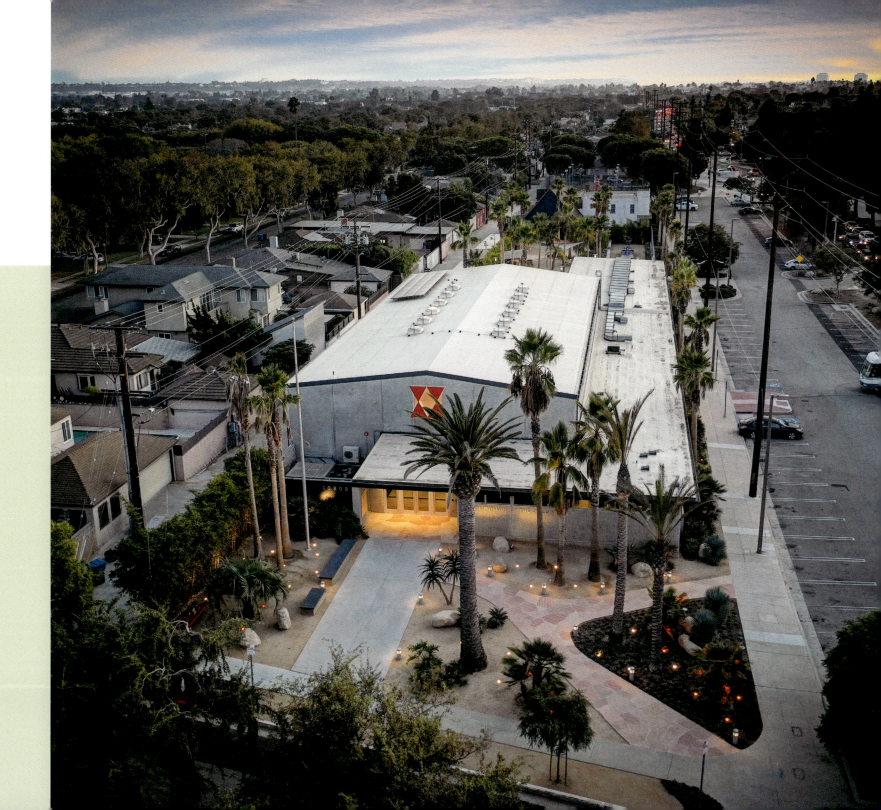

Wende Museum, drawings for phase I + II

Wende Museum II, Glorya Kaufman Center, designed by Michael Boyd and Brian Wickersham of AUX Architecture

Nomadic Constructions: Saving Jean Prouvé

Michael Boyd

As an artisan, self-taught engineer and builder in the French city of Nancy, Jean Prouvé (1901–84) was a hands-on innovator, utilizing sheet metal for furniture and buildings. Through all of these activities his consistent goal was to achieve maximum utility with a minimum of materials at the lowest possible cost.

His furniture was produced in quantity for schools and universities and the revenue subsidized his experiments in prefabrication. Prototypes of his Tropical House were shipped to French colonies in West Africa and flown back to France fifty years later to be restored and widely exhibited.

Thanks largely to the efforts of French gallerist Patrick Seguin, Prouvé has achieved posthumous fame—even cult status—and as a result the demand for original pieces of furniture from Ateliers Prouvé has stimulated a lively trade in fakes and re-issues.

Over the years I've repeatedly combed the flea markets of Paris in search of lost treasures. The most monumental of these finds was Jean Prouvé's *Room 10, École de Dieulouard,* a schoolroom disassembled and brought to the Gustav Eiffel-designed sawtooth roofed warehouses at Clignancourt. Amid the pile-up of generic furniture I spotted an unmistakable pale yellow gleam coming from a stack of sheet-steel beams. Obscured and disheveled as these fragments were, their authenticity jumped out at me. This was one of the many prefabricated structures Prouvé had created over the years; a domestic or commercial version of the Tropical Houses. The elements were shipped to the US, where they were restored and re-assembled with the assistance of architect Alain Baneel.

Prouvé said "there is no difference between the design of a piece of furniture and that of a house." Whether considered as scaled-up case work, cabinetry for living, or micro-architecture, his nomadic architecture is a source of inspiration to every architect and designer who strives for economy infused with poetry. These structures are models of cantilevering, balance, structural strength, and weight distribution, with many logical intricacies to the assembly.

Gaby and I were honored to donate Jean Prouvé's *Room 10, École de Dieulouard* to LACMA. The design and engineering behind these incredible movable buildings is critical to reassess in a contemporary context and the structures must be resurrected and stabilized for use in the 21st century.

Jean Prouvé, *École de Dieulouard | Room 10*

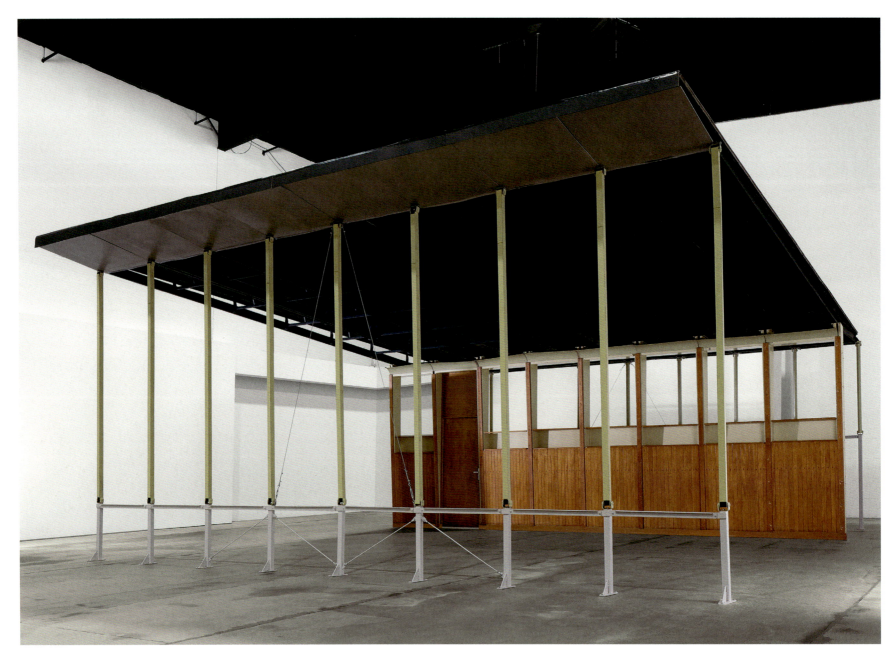

Michael Boyd, drawing for viability, Jean Prouvé,
École de Dieulouard | Room 10

Jean Prouvé, *Standard* chair, c.1930

309

Gabetti and *Isola* stool

310

Green Brown Cream, oil on canvas, 1996

Landscaping Outdoor Rooms

Shed House, 2016, Malibu

Nature's Edges

Michael Boyd

The late Julius Shulman told me that he brought a palm frond in the trunk of his car to every photo shoot. He then would have an assistant hold the greenery in the frame as he shot his iconic images of modernist Los Angeles architecture. The projection of paradise, which the single palm leaf represented to the world, telegraphed the good life, the temperate climate, and the easy/breezy quality of life in post-war southern California.

I also was fascinated to read about Roberto Burle Marx's hikes to find exotic examples of tropical plants. Many of the rare species were then introduced to his own property in Brazil. I have met people who participated in these outings and only wish I could have been there. As a disciple of Burle Marx, I transplanted his idea of the jungle held at bay. The architecture sits among the plants—not the other way around, where the plants merely decorate the building site. Expansive glazing ensures that the garden is *in the house*. The indoor/outdoor principle of the Case Study Program (in accordance with the earlier "Sun Seekers" who came to Los Angeles for their health in the early 20th century, along with Neutra and Schindler) means that you are living *in the garden.*

I'm fascinated by the sculptural beauty of sub-tropical vegetation and its association with modern architecture in an environment where these plants thrive year-round. Los Angeles is a desert, so grass is dishonest and a waste of water. Synthetic grass always looks out of place to me, sometimes comical. However, I am not a formalist about using native plant material in a palette. Naturalism in the final design is certainly the desired effect, but if plants were brought to southern California a century ago and flourished, that is "native" enough for me. Eucalyptus trees, the cypress, and almost every palm, including the Mexican Fan Palm, migrated from around the world and are now respected local citizens.

The California-casual ideal is always in the back of my mind. Overwrought and over-thought hardscapes, plantings installed in too classical an arrangement or plan; these do not work for our garden projects. Constellations of plants obey the same rules as furniture and design objects in an interior, in which elevations are scrambled so as *not* to look man-made. Where and how will trees and plants grow in the future? Where will their canopies end up? What kind of shade or sun does each species desire most?

These are the primary factors that inform the design. Palm trees are mostly self-cleaning and that's a big plus. Pine trees, which need human interaction for trimming and shaping, do not fare well over time. Essentially, I let nature take its course. I try to lightly corral the living organisms into semi-organized zones, occasionally moving specimens if they grow too big, and I replace whatever is dead or dying. Nature's edges are beautiful in their own right. All one has to do is get out of the

Naturalism in the final design is certainly the desired effect, but if plants were brought to southern California a century ago and flourished, that is "native" enough for me.

way and ask the plants, where would they be happiest and who do they want for plant neighbors? Groupings, color contrasts, the employment of decorative rocks, studies of mass and void similar to interiors and architecture, leads the garden experiment to its final layout.

Richard Neutra, who always espoused simplicity in design, created a landscape plan for his Wirin House of 1949, which went unrealized until 2008 when I was brought in by designer and expert Mark Haddawy to create a garden for the house he had recently restored to perfection for the photographer Mark Seliger. Following the Neutra plan, ease and appropriateness were the driving forces for plant material choices; simple outer forms and graphic patterns were selected. The entry garden project was fully realized only after I found, while foraging around in my library, the original Neutra plan in an obscure German periodical. We used the antiquarian tear sheet as gospel, a guide for the new incarnation. Neighbors glowed as they came by, saying "great job!" and I kept responding "it's Neutra's original design." After a while, I gave up on saying anything, as they stared back blankly. They did not need to know who Neutra was, as long as Mark Haddawy and I did.

In addition to Neutra and Burle Marx I follow closely the ideas of Thomas Church and Garrett Eckbo, giants of mid-century modern landscape design. The buildings always feel at home. The plants always feel seen and heard. It is a natural process, like making music. There are dyads and triads, harmony and rhythm.

It is always a goal in my gardens to have the finished design look as if I was never there, much like the building restoration work. I want my participation to appear silent, deferential to nature, always organic, hopefully culminating in an enchanted garden with a strong sense of surprise and delight. If there is design in it—it is nature's natural edges.

John Lautner's Chemosphere House, 1960

PAGES 318–323
Chemosphere House

Shed House, 2016, Malibu

A. Quincy Jones' Nordlinger House #1, 1948, Bel Air

328

Craig Ellwood's Steinman House, 1956, Malibu

Steinman House

Richard Neutra's Wirin House, 1949, Hollywood

John Lautner's Harvey House, 1950, Hollywood

PAGES 338-41
Harvey House

Shift, oil on canvas mounted on wood, 1989

Transcending Trend

Millennium Modern:
Living in Design

Michael Boyd

"Millennium Modern" is a way to describe my work twenty years before and twenty years after the turn of the Millennium. In the summer of 1981 I was captivated when I saw the *Marcel Breuer: Furniture and Interiors* exhibit at MoMA and began collecting vintage modern design—so captivated, in fact, that the visit changed the direction of my life, and up to the present, I am still engaged, having just put the finishing touches on the restoration of A. Quincy Jones' first house for a client, the 1948 Nordlinger House #1. Modernism works for me because it is a philosophy, an approach based on rationality and logic. And, contrary to popular belief, modernism can easily incorporate charm, warmth and femininity. It provides us with a coherent, universal foundation, and allows for adaptability and innovation. While it aims to inspire, the best modernism embraces frailty and human psychology. The philosophy is basic: reduce the elements, use common sense and think of people. More specifically, think of how people will interact with the design, and create beauty through order.

Millennium Modern straddles the bridge between the 20th and 21st centuries – it is universal, eternal, and has been going on for as long as humans have been creating. Across millennia practical and direct path approaches to art and design reoccur all over the world. My focus on 20th century modernism springs from my natural attraction to simplicity and minimalist forms.

What and where is modern? Modern is timeless and geographically widespread. Its central tenet of distilling design to its essence was used in Cycladic Greek figurines, Song Dynasty bowls, and traditional Japanese art and architecture. Modernism can also be used to describe developments in art, architecture and design since the industrial revolution and could be roughly dated 1870-1970. There are many modes of modernism with diverging facets, but certain themes recur: a search for *rationality, honesty, universality, functionality,* and *simplicity*.

There are many practical advantages to living with and in modernism. Two immediate benefits: the impetus to have clear thoughts when inhabiting a clean space, and the inspiration to have provocative thoughts when surrounded with progressive design that challenges you daily.

We need to look again at what made modernism work in its time, and then ask, how does it adapt to our times? Modern can be green, using salvage and vintage. Modern can be made to accommodate up-to-the-minute human needs and desires and incorporate new technologies. It needs to be thought of as a process and not a static goal or look. For me it is an *idée fixe*, an obssession. The modern ideal is not only emblematic of its own time, but acts as a problem-solving model for the future.

> "Great things are not done by impulse, but by a series of small things brought together."
> —Vincent van Gogh

PLANEfurniture Studio, Santa Monica

Five Points Across the Millennium Line

RATIONALITY

"All our knowledge begins with the senses, proceeds then to the understanding, and ends with reason. There is nothing higher than reason." —Immanuel Kant

Modern works because it is based on reason and logic. By approaching design issues in a systemic instead of arbitrary or overly subjective way, we can create calm and order in our living environment. Following grids, systems—even carefully calibrated golden sections—creates frames for living: it appeals to our innate sense of harmony and stability. Modern masters like Le Corbusier and Mies van der Rohe devised intricate measuring systems based on human proportions. Careful calculations were made that were in concert with a person's height, arm reach, and potential movement. When you enter a structure or engage with a piece of furniture that has been devised on this basis, the difference is palpable, even striking.

We live inside design—a house conceived by the Brazilian architect Oscar Niemeyer (the only residence he designed that was built in North America). Although the house has all of the sinuous sensuality of Brazil because of its Santa Monica mountain setting and tropical plantings, it is still strictly within the rectilinear International Style. Our house is filled with furniture and objects that were designed with functional performance in mind, stripped of ornamentation, such as the constructivist designs of Gerrit Rietveld, and minimalist artifacts of the Bauhaus. Being surrounded by such clarity in design thinking not only enhances our daily lives but inspires lucidity. The rationalist frame for living allows for reality—for life to be naturally messy yet contained.

HONESTY

"The truth is more important than the facts."
—Frank Lloyd Wright

The best modernism does not use trickery or ring false in any way. It's not a question of purity only, but of appropriateness; more than exhaustive analysis, using modern as a model requires a meter for truth, taste and common sense. Honesty also doesn't mean using only organic (as opposed to man-made) materials. The point is that the use of materials—wood, metal, stone, or even plastic and resin—be guided by the way they were intended to be used; minimum expression towards maximum capability.

Honest engineering revealed is uplifting and stimulating. Honest architecture and design have nothing to hide. Structures are often exposed, not just for philosophical reasons, but also in order to achieve aesthetically pleasing end products. The Eames House of 1950, with its prefabricated, modular, industrial parts, is a manifesto of honesty in construction. In fact, the original design that the parts were ordered for was abandoned, and the actual buildings (house and studio) were made by rearranging the already-on-site panels and structural rails. The Rietveld Schroeder House of 1924, for all of its intricacy and flexibility, never deceives or misleads. In both cases, the buildings never belie their own making; as Frank Stella said about his earliest constructivist paintings, "What you see is what you see." When one is not distracted or confused by the separate component parts of a design, but takes in the unified design in totality, one senses the integrity and feels the resolution.

UNIVERSALITY
"Today we all speak, if not the same tongue, the same universal language."—Octavio Paz

Seeking the universal is an age-old pursuit. In art, music and literature, timelessness is the highest goal. Since its inception at the beginning of the 20th century, the focus of modernist architecture has been to create housing and apartment dwellings that are repeatable models. The *Weissenhofsiedlung*, a model housing exhibition of 1927 in Stuttgart that utilized the talents of Mies, Le Corbusier and Walter Gropius, comprised dwellings that could be replicated in other places and times. The *Case Study Program* in mid-century Los Angeles set out to revolutionize home design

Shed House, 2016, Malibu; *Floating Planes*, 2013

OPPOSITE
Comstock Apartment, 1961, San Francisco: *House Paint Diptych*, 2010; Jean Prouvé, *EM* table, 1950

for the new post-war era. John Entenza, publisher of the influential *Arts & Architecture* magazine which sponsored the program, recruited some of the best southern California architects of the time to create reiterations of dwellings (although, as realized, the program became more bespoke). Modernity is the presence of the present. Universalism includes the past. Modernist ideology denounces lethargy and complacency in design. It always stands for social advancement. Theoretically, reason will lead to universal truths all cultures will embrace. Western society in the 19th century, with its caked on layers, paved the way for modernism and its progressive point of view. Dishonesty in materials, unnecessarily ornate design, and general relativism gave way to logic and reason in the simultaneous pursuit of beauty and function. It is not a question of now or new with modernism, as much as it is the boiling down to the essence of a design or idea, the seeking of the omnipresent truth.

FUNCTIONALITY
"Who ever said that pleasure wasn't functional?"
—Charles Eames

The best modernism is predicated on functionality—the editing and paring down to the essence of a design. As Louis Sullivan famously declared in 1896, "form follows function."

The Dutch modernist J.J.P. Oud practiced a clean-lined, no-frills style that was founded on functionalism. In his own words, his art was "poetic functionalism"—he hoped to merge scientific concerns with the expectations of the users. His *Municipal Housing* in Rotterdam (1918–33) serviced many workers and was a socially conscious effort to bring efficient functioning to the foreground. The *Modular Series* (1950) furniture designs of Charles and Ray Eames for Herman Miller are purely functional, showing the Miesian principle in action. All parts of the interchangeable chairs must withstand heavy use; the modularity of the furniture line also contributes to their usefulness in multiple contexts, from airports to barber shops, from jazz musicians' humble homes to top designers' lairs. Design's deepest beauty is defined by its widest use.

Functionality is not so much an exercise meant to purify, but more accurately *to distill* the architectural and aesthetic ideas. If you don't need another part or new idea to make something work effortlessly, leave it out. The act of distillation in design can create a serenity and quiet that permeates interior space, that can silence massive architectural structures, and lend peacefulness to gardens. Furniture in our personal collection could be classified as "functionalism from all eras." Jean Prouvé wanted to make engineering evident. Poul Kjaerholm, Charles and Ray Eames, and Marcel Breuer, were more focused on utility than utopia. The earliest

OPPOSITE
Wende Museum, Culver City

THIS PAGE
Johnston Marklee, Chan Luu House, Hawaii: Flip; Lounge chairs, 2012

example of functionalism in modernism is Thonet bentwood furniture (circa 1870), which the filmmaker Billy Wilder collected himself, and used in many of his movie sets to telegraph "progressive is beautiful."

SIMPLICITY
"Simplicity is the ultimate form of sophistication."
—Leonardo Da Vinci

The modernist concept of simplicity revolves around the elimination of unnecessary decoration or detail. Most often by subtracting elements one is adding to the power of the overall effect. The art of reduction can slow down and soothe a garden design as well as a building or piece of furniture. A tone is set with simplicity for meditative living—but not tranquilizing; clarity and directness can be simultaneously energizing.

Philip Johnson's Glass House of 1949, in contrast to much of the architect's unnecessarily complex later work, is the ultimate minimal dwelling. Gerrit Rietveld's *Zig-Zag Chair* of 1934 is a perfect expression of seating reduced to the most basic elements of back, seat, and support. In profile, the chair is practically invisible, a line drawing come-to-life. Practicing the art of reduction, and making man's environments simple, legible, clear and calm, creates space for living, a feeling of freedom from the stresses of life.

Gropius' Bauhaus ideal migrated from Europe across the globe—eventually landing at the end of Route 66 at America's west coast, in Los Angeles. The City of Angels is both the beginning of a new world and a continuation of the old. You can see the coexistence. Leaving out ornament, focusing on the fundamental, glorifying the basic—this was the concept for *Arts & Architecture* and its Case Study Program. The most pristine forms of residential architecture sit in southern California next to the most frantic and far-fetched spec-homes and mega-mansions. The contrast between the underwhelming and overwhelming is conspicuous. Clean and quiet architectural design wins any side-by-side comparison with the rambling fortresses.

Continuum
A conclusion is the end of the line so I would rather talk in terms of the beginning of a new millennium line. The modern approach to design and living is well represented on both sides, a continuum across the endless time line. Modern is eternal. Many ancient cultures practiced minimalist art, just as contemporary artists sometimes try to infuse their works with dreamed up layers of history for texture and a sense of authenticity. The best modernist architecture—such as Le Corbusier's Villa Savoye (1928-31), and Mies' Farnsworth House (1951)—is timeless because it appeals to our innate

sense of unity and order, like the ancient architecture of Egypt. The pinnacle of modernist design—such as the sheet steel furniture of Jean Prouvé, and the fiberglass chairs of Charles and Ray Eames—works because it takes into consideration its functionality and follows these rationalist precepts in their execution. They are a delight because they work physically, as in cradling your body, while pleasing the eye and the mind because they are modest, original ideas that work. This is because of their revealed structure and honesty—both Prouvé and Eames are examples of engineering made visible. A similar approach is critical when restoring works of architecture. The best modernist restoration blends seamlessly with the preexisting, extending existing elegantly laid out systems. I personally feel I have been very fortunate to be able to interact with historic modern houses, to learn from them, and have the opportunity to analyze what makes them such noteworthy stand-outs. Living in design, dwelling in art and architecture elevates the senses, nothing less.

Modern is still here. It has always been here—even before we knew what to call it. It was a vital force in past millennia in the form of cave paintings and tribal art and is still a relevant and revitalizing model for design solutions in the present millennium. Why is the spirit and ethos of mid-century modernism still important this century? Simplicity transcends trend.

Nordlinger House #1, garden detail

Chemosphere House, garden detail

Acknowledgments

Special thanks to Gabrielle Doré Boyd.

I would also like to thank Roman Alonso, Simon and Melanie Andrews, Paola Antonelli, Elizabeth Armstrong, Albert and Holly Baril, Aaron Betsky, Dorothy Bourne, Matthew Bourne, Laurel Broughton, Edward Cella, Joel Chen, Kristan Cunningham, Mario DeLopez, Ava Doré, Jennifer Fletcher Dunlop, Hans Eckhardt, Lisa Eisner, Ken Erwin, Christopher Farr, Thom Faulders, Adrienne Fish, Scott Frances, Steve Freihon, Phillipe Garner, Linda Gershon, Jocelyn Gibbs, Mitch Glaser, Dalton Gomez, Mark Grotjahn, Jennifer Guidi, Andy Hackman, Mark Haddawy, Mark Hennessey, Sarah Herda, Thomas S. Hines, Brooke Hodge, Mick Hodgson, Harry and Maria Hopper, Grant Irish, Justin Jampol, Scott Jarrell, Peter Jefferson, Steven Johannknecht, Sharon Johnston, Daren Joy, Alba Kane, Michael Maharam, Marina Mills Kitchen, Eric Lamers, Mark Lee, Kelly Lynch, Jennifer Mahanay, Mark McDonald, Giovanni Mercado, Lars Müller, Lynn Pickwell, Richard Powers, Joe Rainsford, Oscar and Elena Saldana, Dave Shaw, Robert Zin Stark, Eric Staudenmaier, William Stout, Benedikt Taschen, Michael Webb, Lorraine Wild, Leslie Williamson, Doug Woods, Richard Wright and James Zemaitis.
—MB

ABOVE
ROD series, *Flip Lounge* chairs and ottomans, *Shed House*, 2016, Malibu

PHOTOGRAPHER CREDITS
Front Cover Photograph: Richard Powers
Back Cover Photograph: Matthew Momberger
Patrik Argast: Pages 1–5, 174–180, 187–193, 195–199, 202–204, 206–211, 214–217, 219–229
Adrian Gaut: Pages 6, 205, 345
Mariko Reed: Pages 8–9
Scott Frances: Pages 14, 116–129
Steve Freihon: Pages 17–23
Matthew Momberger: Pages 26–45, 326–327
Jakob Elliot: Pages 46–61, 84
Richard Powers: Pages 62–73, 83, 85–107, 133, 136–138, 140–141, 144–147, 150–151, 154–155, 157–159, 162–165, 167, 168–169, 330–331, 346–347
Hans Eckardt: Pages 74–81, 182, 212–213, 218, 236–251, 317–325, 332–341, 350, 352
Jim Bartsch: Pages 108–115
Eric Staudenmaier: Pages 134–135, 139, 142–143, 148–149, 153, 156, 160–161, 166
Sam Frost: Page 173
Spencer Lowell: Pages 194, 258–271
James O. Davies: Page 232
Stephen Kent Johnson: Pages 234–235, 256, 252–253
Trevor Tondro: Page 255
William Waldron: Page 257
Ian Reeves: Pages 274–279
Florian Holzherr: Pages 286–287

MICHAEL BOYD
Michael Boyd is a furniture, landscape, interior and architectural designer based in Los Angeles. He is the principal of BoydDesign, a consultancy for the restoration and preservation of modernist architecture, and for collecting modern art and design. His most notable restorations include Paul Rudolph's Rudolph Townhouse (1975) in New York City; Oscar Niemeyer's Strick House (1964) in Santa Monica, this architect's only built work in North America besides the U.N. complex; and Craig Ellwood's Steinman House (1956) in Malibu. Boyd is the founder of and designer for PLANEfurniture, a line of architectural furnishings, examples of which have been selected for the permanent collections of SFMOMA, The Palm Springs Museum, and the UCSB Gebhard Art + Architecture Archives. He is an internationally renowned collector and a widely published expert on 20th-century design and post-war modernism.

MICHAEL WEBB
Michael Webb, Hon. AIA/LA, worked as a journalist and editor in London, moved to Washington DC in 1969 to direct programming for the American Film Institute, and then to Los Angeles, where he lives in a classic Richard Neutra apartment that was formerly home to Charles and Ray Eames. He is the author of more than 25 books, most recently *Architects' Houses, Moving Around: A Lifetime of Wandering*, and *Building Community: New Apartment Architecture*. In addition, he has contributed essays to many monographs as well as studies of work by Frank Gehry, Tadao Ando, Richard Meier and Norman Foster. Webb travels the world to gather material for contributions to *Architectural Record, The Architectural Review* (including guest-edited issues on China and Colombia), *A+U, The Plan, Wallpaper* and *World of Interiors*.

First published in 2022 by Lund Humphries

Lund Humphries
Office 3, Book House
261A City Road
London EC1V 1JX
UK

www.lundhumphries.com

Millennium Modern: Living in Design
© Michael Boyd, 2022
All rights reserved

ISBN: 978-1-84822-602-9

A Cataloguing-in-Publication record for this book is available from the British Library

All rights reserved. No part of this publication may be reproduced, stored in a retrieval system or transmitted in any form or by any means, electrical, mechanical or otherwise, without first seeking the permission of the copyright owners and publishers. Every effort has been made to seek permission to reproduce the images in this book. Any omissions are entirely unintentional, and details should be addressed to the publishers.

Michael Boyd has asserted his right under the Copyright, Designs and Patent Act, 1988, to be identified as the Author of this Work.

Designed by Lorraine Wild and Tommy Huang, Green Dragon Office
Set in Gerstner Programm
Printed in Belgium